Chapter 1: Introduction to RF and Electromagnetic Waves

Overview of Radio Frequency (RF) and Its Importance in Communication Systems

Radio Frequency (RF) refers to the electromagnetic wave frequencies that fall within the range of approximately 3 kHz to 300 GHz. RF waves are widely used for transmitting information over distances through wireless communication systems. These waves are the cornerstone of modern telecommunications, including radio, television, cellular networks, Wi-Fi, and satellite communication.

The importance of RF in communication systems cannot be overstated. RF is the medium through which signals are transmitted and received in various communication technologies, enabling everything from basic two-way radios to advanced 5G mobile networks. These waves are harnessed in many different applications, ranging from simple voice communications to complex data transfer and location-based services.

A deeper understanding of RF and its behavior is essential for designing and maintaining these systems. The efficiency and reliability of wireless communication depend on the proper management of RF signals, ensuring minimal interference and optimal signal quality. RF communication systems are subject to environmental factors, system design limitations, and external interference, all of which need to be addressed to maintain high-quality service.

Electromagnetic Spectrum and Basic Principles

The electromagnetic spectrum refers to the range of all possible frequencies of electromagnetic radiation. This spectrum includes a wide range of wave frequencies, from extremely low-frequency waves used in power transmission, to extremely high-frequency waves used in x-rays and gamma rays. RF waves are a subset of the electromagnetic spectrum, situated between the low-frequency waves (used in power distribution) and the microwave and infrared bands.

The behavior of electromagnetic waves follows several basic principles:

1. **Wave Propagation**: Electromagnetic waves, including RF signals, propagate through space, transferring energy from one point to another. These waves can travel through different mediums (air, vacuum, or cables) depending on their frequency and the design of the communication system.

2. **Wave Properties**: RF waves exhibit the properties of all electromagnetic waves, including wavelength, frequency, amplitude, and phase. These properties influence the design of antennas, signal transmission, and reception. The wavelength is inversely proportional to the frequency, with higher frequencies corresponding to shorter wavelengths.

3. **Energy Transmission**: RF waves carry energy, which is used to encode and transmit information over distances. This transmission can either be in the form of analog or digital signals, depending on the communication system's design.

4. **Interference and Reflection**: RF signals are susceptible to interference from other sources of electromagnetic radiation and can also reflect off surfaces, leading to signal degradation. These factors must be considered when designing communication systems to ensure that the transmitted signals are strong, clear, and free from external interference.

Types of Signals and Their Applications in Everyday Life

RF signals are used in a wide variety of applications, and understanding their types is crucial for mastering RF jamming, electromagnetic interference (EMI), and shielding. The key types of signals in RF communication include:

1. **Analog Signals**: Analog RF signals continuously vary in amplitude, frequency, or phase, and they are commonly used in older communication technologies, such as AM/FM radio broadcasts. Analog signals are more susceptible to interference and distortion, which makes them less efficient for modern communication systems.

2. **Digital Signals**: Digital RF signals are used to transmit data in the form of binary code (ones and zeros). These signals are less prone to noise and interference compared to analog signals and are widely used in technologies like Wi-Fi, cellular networks, and digital television.

3. **Modulated Signals**: Modulation is the process of varying a carrier wave's amplitude, frequency, or phase to encode information. The most common types of modulation used in RF communication are Amplitude Modulation (AM), Frequency Modulation (FM), and Phase Modulation (PM). More advanced techniques such as Frequency Hopping Spread Spectrum (FHSS) and Code Division Multiple Access (CDMA) are also used in modern communication systems to improve reliability and security.

4. **Pulse Signals**: Pulse signals consist of brief bursts of RF energy and are often used in radar, satellite communication, and certain types of wireless communication systems. Pulse modulation allows for efficient use of bandwidth and is a key feature of systems such as radar, where the transmission is intermittent but must still cover a wide area.

5. **Carrier Signals**: Carrier signals are used to carry information over RF waves. These signals are typically modulated with data and can be continuous or intermittent, depending on the type of communication system.

Applications of RF signals are ubiquitous in daily life. Here are a few examples:

- **Cellular Networks**: RF signals are the backbone of mobile communications. They enable voice calls, text messages, and internet access via mobile devices. Modern cellular networks use multiple frequencies across various bands, such as 4G LTE and 5G, to provide fast and reliable service to users.
- **Wi-Fi**: Wireless networking protocols, such as Wi-Fi, use RF signals to enable devices to connect to local area networks without physical cables. Wi-Fi operates typically within the 2.4 GHz and 5 GHz bands, allowing for data transfer at high speeds.
- **Television and Radio Broadcasting**: RF signals have been used for decades to transmit analog and digital television and radio broadcasts. These broadcasts are received by antennas and converted back into audio and video signals for consumer use.
- **GPS and Navigation Systems**: GPS systems rely on RF signals transmitted from satellites to provide location data to users. These signals are received by GPS devices and used to calculate precise geographic locations.
- **Radar Systems**: Radar systems use RF waves to detect objects and measure their distance, speed, and direction. This technology is widely used in air traffic control, weather monitoring, military applications, and automotive systems like collision detection and adaptive cruise control.

- **Bluetooth and Other Short-Range Communication Technologies**: Bluetooth technology, which operates in the 2.4 GHz ISM band, enables devices to communicate wirelessly over short distances. It is used in applications ranging from wireless headsets and speakers to IoT devices.

Conclusion

Radio Frequency (RF) and electromagnetic waves play a central role in modern communication systems, facilitating everything from cellular networks to satellite communication. Understanding the properties of RF waves, the behavior of electromagnetic signals, and their applications in everyday life is crucial for mastering topics like RF jamming, electromagnetic interference (EMI), RF shielding, and signal suppression.

In the chapters that follow, we will explore these subjects in detail, focusing on how RF jamming and EMI can disrupt communication systems, the techniques used to mitigate these issues, and the importance of RF shielding and signal suppression in maintaining reliable, high-performance systems. This foundational knowledge is essential for anyone working in the field of RF technology, from communication engineers to cybersecurity experts, as well as those interested in the cutting-edge developments that are shaping the future of wireless communication.

Chapter 2: Basics of RF Jamming
Definition and History of RF Jamming

RF jamming is the deliberate transmission of electromagnetic signals to disrupt or block the normal operation of communication systems. It involves the generation of radio frequency signals designed to interfere with, degrade, or completely deny the legitimate operation of RF communication systems. By overpowering the target system's signals with noise or other forms of interference, RF jamming can disrupt critical communications, rendering the affected systems ineffective.

Historically, RF jamming has been associated with military operations, where it is used as a form of electronic warfare to neutralize enemy communication systems. During World War II, jamming was first used in earnest by the Allies to disrupt the Nazi radar systems and prevent them from detecting incoming bombers. Since then, RF jamming has evolved into a more sophisticated technology with a wide range of applications, both in military and civilian contexts.

In the 20th century, the proliferation of RF-based communication technologies, such as radios, satellite systems, and cellular networks, expanded the scope of jamming operations. As global reliance on wireless communication grew, so did the need to address the potential for interference from jamming devices. With the rise of mobile phones, GPS systems, and Wi-Fi networks, RF jamming techniques became more varied and complex, leading to the development of countermeasures and regulations to limit the impact of deliberate interference.

How RF Jamming Works: Principles and Techniques

RF jamming works by intentionally transmitting a signal that interferes with the legitimate signals used by communication systems. The disruption can take several forms, depending on the type of jamming and the target system. The core principle behind RF jamming is the overpowering of the target signal, preventing it from reaching its intended destination or disrupting the system's ability to function properly.

There are two primary ways that RF jamming can work:

1. **Noise Jamming**: This involves broadcasting a random or continuous signal at the same frequency as the target communication system. The noise overwhelms the desired signal, causing communication failure or severe degradation in signal quality. Noise jamming can be broadband, affecting a wide range of frequencies, or narrowband, targeting specific frequency bands used by the communication system.

2. **Deceptive Jamming**: Instead of simply overpowering the target signal with noise, deceptive jamming involves injecting misleading signals into the system to cause the receiver to misinterpret the information. For example, in radar jamming, a false echo could be sent to make a radar system think an object is present when it is not, or conversely, to make it think an object is not present when it is.

Other techniques may involve **spot jamming**, where interference is focused on a specific frequency, or **sweeping jamming**, where the interference moves across a range of frequencies to prevent the target from locking onto a particular channel.

Jamming can be further classified based on the level of sophistication:

- **Analog Jamming**: Early forms of jamming involved simply generating continuous waves of interference. These jamming techniques were often indiscriminate and crude but could still effectively block certain communications.
- **Digital Jamming**: Modern jammers use digital signal processing (DSP) to create more complex, adaptive forms of interference. These jammers are capable of targeting specific communication protocols and modulations, making them more effective against advanced communication systems.

Types of Jamming Signals

Jamming signals can be broadly categorized into different types, each with distinct characteristics. The choice of jamming signal depends on the target system and the goals of the jamming operation.

1. **Narrowband Jamming**: Narrowband jamming occurs when the interference is focused on a small portion of the frequency spectrum, typically targeting the frequency band used by the target communication system. This type of jamming is most effective when the target system operates within a narrow range of frequencies, such as a specific radio frequency channel or communication band.

2. **Wideband Jamming**: In contrast to narrowband jamming, wideband jamming involves broadcasting interference across a broader range of frequencies. This type of jamming can affect multiple communication systems that use different frequency bands. While wideband jamming can be more disruptive, it is often less precise than narrowband jamming, as it may not be focused on the exact frequency of the target system.

3. **Pulse Jamming**: Pulse jamming involves the transmission of short bursts of high-power interference at specific intervals. This type of jamming can be highly effective against radar systems or systems that rely on pulse modulation, as it disrupts the timing and synchronization of the signals.

4. **Deceptive Jamming**: Deceptive jamming, also known as "spoofing," involves sending false or misleading signals to confuse the target system. This type of jamming can mislead receivers into interpreting false data, such as incorrectly identifying the location of a vehicle or aircraft. Deceptive jamming is often used in military or defense applications to disrupt radar systems and misguide enemy operations.

5. **Denying Jamming**: This type of jamming aims to completely block communication by overpowering the legitimate signal to such an extent that the system cannot function. Denying jamming can render communication systems unusable until the jamming ceases or the system can be re-established on a different frequency.

6. **Spot Jamming**: Spot jamming involves targeting a specific frequency or small frequency band. It is a precise form of interference that focuses on disrupting the communication of a particular system, like a cellular phone, Wi-Fi device, or GPS signal.

7. **Sweep Jamming**: Sweep jamming, also known as frequency hopping jamming, is designed to jam a wide range of frequencies by continuously shifting the interference signal across different frequency bands. This method is effective against systems that use frequency-hopping techniques, such as military communication systems.

Applications and Scenarios for RF Jamming

RF jamming has a variety of applications, most of which are related to interference, disruption, and denial of communication. Some of the key scenarios where RF jamming is applied include:

1. **Military Operations**: RF jamming has been used extensively in military operations to disrupt enemy communications and radar systems. By disabling the enemy's communication network, jammers can provide a strategic advantage on the battlefield. Modern military jamming devices are capable of targeting various communication systems, including satellite communications, GPS, and radar.

2. **Electronic Warfare**: In the realm of electronic warfare, RF jamming plays a crucial role in neutralizing hostile radar systems, preventing guided missiles from targeting accurately, and impairing the navigation capabilities of enemy aircraft. Jammers are used to protect friendly forces and disrupt enemy activities.

3. **Civilian Applications**: In some cases, RF jamming is used in civilian contexts. For example, it may be used to prevent unauthorized communication in secure areas, such as prisons or military installations. Jamming can also be used to block malicious or illegal communications, such as the use of cell phones in restricted areas.

4. **Countermeasures and Anti-Jamming Technology**: As RF jamming becomes more sophisticated, systems are developed to counteract jamming attempts. Anti-jamming techniques, such as frequency hopping, spread spectrum communication, and encryption, are employed to protect communication systems from interference. These technologies make it more difficult for jammers to successfully disrupt signals.

5. **Commercial and Public Safety Use**: In some regions, RF jamming is used for public safety purposes, such as blocking signals from cellular networks in locations like courtrooms or government buildings where unauthorized communication could pose a threat. However, the use of jamming in civilian areas is highly regulated due to its potential to disrupt legitimate communications.

Conclusion

RF jamming is a powerful technique used to intentionally disrupt or deny communication systems by introducing interference into the radio frequency spectrum. The principles of jamming involve the generation of disruptive signals that overpower or deceive the intended signals of communication systems. Understanding the various types of jamming signals, their techniques, and applications provides a foundation for tackling the challenges of RF jamming in both military and civilian contexts.

In the next chapters, we will delve deeper into how RF jamming interacts with electromagnetic interference (EMI), explore mitigation strategies, and discuss the technologies used for shielding and suppression to ensure reliable communication in an increasingly complex electromagnetic environment.

Chapter 3: Understanding Electromagnetic Interference (EMI)

EMI and Its Sources (Natural and Artificial)

Electromagnetic Interference (EMI) is the disturbance or degradation of the performance of an electrical or electronic device due to electromagnetic radiation emitted from an external source. This interference can cause malfunctions, data corruption, or complete system failure. EMI can be caused by both natural and artificial sources, making it a complex and ever-present challenge in the design, operation, and maintenance of communication systems.

Natural sources of EMI include:

1. **Solar Activity**: The Sun emits a wide range of electromagnetic radiation, including X-rays and ultraviolet radiation, which can affect satellite communication systems and GPS receivers. Solar flares and coronal mass ejections (CMEs) are powerful events that can disrupt communication systems on Earth.
2. **Lightning**: Lightning strikes produce electromagnetic pulses (EMPs) that can induce high-voltage surges in electrical systems. This can damage sensitive electronics and disrupt communications over large geographical areas.
3. **Cosmic Radiation**: High-energy particles from outer space can interfere with electronic systems, particularly those that operate in space or at high altitudes. This is a key concern for satellite communication systems and high-altitude aviation.

Artificial sources of EMI are far more prevalent and can come from a wide range of devices and systems:

1. **Power Lines**: High-voltage power lines emit electromagnetic radiation, which can cause interference with nearby communication equipment, especially if the equipment is not properly shielded or grounded.

2. **Electrical Appliances**: Everyday electronic devices, such as motors, power supplies, and fluorescent lights, can generate EMI that affects nearby equipment. These devices emit electromagnetic radiation, especially during their operation.

3. **Industrial Machinery**: Large machines and motors, used in manufacturing and automation, are significant sources of EMI. The operation of heavy electrical equipment like welding machines, induction furnaces, and electrical generators can disrupt communication systems if they are not properly designed with EMI mitigation techniques.

4. **Computers and Consumer Electronics**: With the proliferation of electronic devices, the amount of EMI generated by consumer electronics has increased significantly. Devices such as cell phones, routers, and laptops, as well as home entertainment systems, can emit EMI that affects other devices in their proximity.

5. **Communication Systems**: Even communication systems themselves can be sources of EMI. In complex communication networks, interference may come from multiple transmitting devices, including radio towers, cell towers, Wi-Fi routers, and satellite communication terminals. These devices can interfere with each other if not carefully managed.

The Science Behind EMI: How Electromagnetic Waves Cause Interference

EMI arises when electromagnetic waves interact with electronic devices in ways that disrupt their normal operation. At its core, the process involves the emission of unwanted electromagnetic energy (the interference) into the electromagnetic spectrum, where it interacts with nearby systems.

Electromagnetic waves, like RF signals, consist of electric and magnetic fields that propagate through space. When an RF signal, or any electromagnetic wave, strikes an electronic device, it can induce unwanted voltages or currents that disrupt the operation of the device. The effects can vary from minor signal degradation to complete equipment failure, depending on the intensity and frequency of the interference.

There are several ways in which EMI affects devices:

1. **Inductive Coupling**: When a device emits electromagnetic energy, this energy can induce a current in nearby conductors. If the interference signal is strong enough, it can affect the normal functioning of the conductors within the affected system, resulting in data corruption or system malfunction.

2. **Capacitive Coupling**: Electromagnetic fields can also induce unwanted voltage across the insulation of electronic circuits. When this happens, the voltage can disrupt the normal operation of sensitive components, such as semiconductors or integrated circuits.

3. **Radiated Emissions**: High-frequency RF emissions can be radiated from electronic equipment or cables. These emissions can spread into the surrounding environment and cause interference with nearby systems, especially those operating in similar frequency bands.

4. **Conducted Emissions**: In some cases, EMI is not radiated into the air but instead travels through power or signal cables, entering other equipment through their connections to the affected system. This is known as conducted EMI and is typically more difficult to control, as the interference follows the electrical path of the system.

5. **Resonance**: Devices and cables have natural resonant frequencies at which they are most susceptible to electromagnetic energy. When an external signal matches or comes close to a device's resonant frequency, the intensity of the interference is amplified, leading to more significant disruptions.

Types of EMI: Conducted, Radiated, and Magnetic

EMI can be broadly categorized into three types based on how the interference is transmitted and where it originates:

1. **Conducted EMI**: Conducted EMI refers to interference that is transferred via electrical conductors, such as power lines or cables. In this case, the electromagnetic energy flows through the cables into other devices, causing interference. Conducted EMI is typically more difficult to mitigate because it can travel long distances through the electrical wiring. To reduce this type of interference, devices must be equipped with filters and grounding mechanisms that block or divert the EMI from sensitive circuits.

2. **Radiated EMI**: Radiated EMI occurs when electromagnetic waves are emitted into the air and propagate through space. This type of interference can affect any nearby system that is sensitive to electromagnetic waves in the same frequency range. Radiated EMI can be controlled using shielding materials, enclosures, and antennas designed to absorb or block the energy.

3. **Magnetic EMI**: Magnetic EMI is a form of interference that is caused by fluctuating magnetic fields. This type of EMI can have a significant impact on devices like transformers, motors, and power supplies, which operate using alternating current (AC) and generate magnetic fields as part of their normal operation. Magnetic fields can also induce current in nearby circuits, affecting their performance. Magnetic shielding or the use of inductive components can help mitigate magnetic EMI.

Real-World Examples of EMI in Various Industries

EMI can disrupt communication, manufacturing, transportation, healthcare, and many other industries. Below are some real-world examples where EMI has caused significant issues:

1. **Aerospace and Aviation**: In the aerospace industry, EMI is a critical concern, especially for navigation and communication systems in aircraft. Electromagnetic interference from weather radar, communication devices, and even onboard electronic equipment can disrupt the operation of sensitive avionics. A notable example is the interference caused by electromagnetic radiation from engines or other electronic equipment that can disrupt navigation systems, leading to potential safety hazards.

2. **Medical Devices**: Medical devices, such as pacemakers, defibrillators, and MRI machines, rely on sensitive electronics to perform critical functions. EMI from nearby mobile phones, radio signals, or electrical equipment can lead to the malfunction of these life-saving devices. Hospitals and medical facilities often implement stringent EMI protection measures to safeguard patient health and ensure the reliability of medical devices.

3. **Automotive Industry**: Modern vehicles are equipped with a wide range of electronic systems, from GPS navigation and infotainment systems to advanced driver assistance systems (ADAS). EMI from onboard equipment or external sources can disrupt vehicle communication systems, affecting safety and performance. In some cases, EMI has been known to interfere with the operation of airbags, anti-lock braking systems (ABS), and electronic stability control (ESC), potentially leading to serious safety issues.

4. **Telecommunications**: The telecommunications industry is particularly vulnerable to EMI, as it depends on the clear transmission of RF signals over various frequencies. Cell towers, satellite systems, and wireless networks are all subject to EMI from neighboring devices. Interference can lead to dropped calls, poor signal quality, or complete communication failure, which can affect both commercial and emergency services.

5. **Consumer Electronics**: Everyday electronic devices, such as smartphones, televisions, and laptops, can emit EMI that disrupts the operation of other nearby devices. For instance, EMI from a router can interfere with the functioning of a nearby television set, resulting in distorted images or signal loss. To mitigate these issues, manufacturers employ EMI shielding and grounding techniques in product design.

Conclusion

Electromagnetic Interference (EMI) is a pervasive issue that affects a wide range of industries and systems. It can arise from both natural and artificial sources and can manifest as conducted, radiated, or magnetic interference. Understanding the science behind EMI and its impact on electronic systems is crucial for designing resilient communication systems, ensuring device reliability, and mitigating the risks associated with interference.

As we move into the next chapters, we will explore the impact of EMI on communication systems, methods of controlling and reducing EMI, and how RF shielding and signal suppression techniques can be applied to ensure optimal system performance and reliability.

Chapter 4: The Impact of EMI on Communication Systems

Effects of EMI on Wireless Communication Systems

Electromagnetic Interference (EMI) is a pervasive and often disruptive force that can significantly degrade the performance of wireless communication systems. Wireless communication systems rely on the transmission and reception of electromagnetic signals, typically in the form of radio frequencies (RF). These systems are designed to operate within specific frequency bands, and any disturbance in these bands can lead to communication failure, signal degradation, or loss of data integrity.

EMI affects wireless communication systems in several ways:

1. **Signal Degradation**: EMI can distort the integrity of the transmitted signal, resulting in reduced signal-to-noise ratios (SNR). When the desired signal is obscured by noise from interfering signals, it becomes harder for the receiver to distinguish the valid information from the unwanted noise. This can lead to fuzzy audio, poor video quality, or corrupted data in the case of digital systems.
2. **Dropped Connections**: For systems that rely on continuous communication, such as cellular networks, Wi-Fi, or satellite communications, EMI can cause dropped connections. This is especially problematic for real-time applications like voice calls, video conferencing, or streaming services, where even brief interruptions can disrupt the user experience.
3. **Reduced Range**: EMI can also affect the effective range of wireless communication systems. As the interference increases, the system may struggle to maintain a reliable connection at a given distance. This can be especially critical in applications like GPS navigation or emergency communication systems where range and reliability are paramount.
4. **Data Loss**: In digital communication systems, EMI can lead to data corruption. Signals can be misinterpreted due to the introduction of noise, causing errors in data packets or even complete loss of data. This is particularly damaging in systems that rely on accurate and high-volume data transmission, such as network communication or automated industrial control systems.

5. **Bandwidth Reduction**: EMI may force communication systems to operate at lower frequencies or reduce their data transmission speeds in order to avoid interference. This is especially true in systems that use wideband or high-frequency signals. As a result, the overall efficiency and performance of the communication network are compromised.

How EMI Degrades Performance in RF Equipment

Radio Frequency (RF) equipment is highly sensitive to interference, and the performance of such devices is directly influenced by the presence of EMI. RF equipment, which includes radio transceivers, antennas, amplifiers, and receivers, operates by transmitting and receiving electromagnetic waves. When EMI is introduced into the environment, it can cause a range of detrimental effects on the performance of RF systems.

1. **Intermodulation Distortion**: When two or more electromagnetic signals mix within an RF system, intermodulation distortion (IMD) can occur. This results in the creation of unwanted frequencies that were not present in the original signals, often leading to the generation of spurious signals or harmonics that interfere with the desired transmission. Intermodulation is a common form of distortion caused by EMI in multi-frequency systems.

2. **Phase Noise**: Phase noise refers to rapid, short-term variations in the phase of the signal. EMI can introduce phase shifts that cause phase noise in the signal, leading to poor signal synchronization, reduced clarity, and errors in timing. In high-precision communication systems, such as radar or satellite communications, phase noise can seriously impair system accuracy and reliability.

3. **Amplifier Overload**: RF amplifiers are designed to amplify weak signals to a level suitable for transmission. However, when EMI is introduced, it can cause the amplifier to become overloaded, distorting the amplified signal. This results in signal clipping or saturation, which significantly reduces the overall quality of the transmitted signal.

4. **Antenna Interference**: Antennas, which are designed to receive and transmit electromagnetic waves, can become susceptible to EMI. Interference can lead to misalignment in the antenna's receiving pattern, reducing the system's ability to capture weak signals or causing the antenna to pick up unwanted signals from nearby sources.

5. **Receiver Desensitization**: In an RF communication system, receivers are tuned to specific frequencies to pick up the desired signals. EMI can desensitize the receiver by introducing noise at these target frequencies, making it harder for the receiver to detect the desired signal amidst the interference. This can lead to poor reception, distortion, or even complete loss of signal.

EMI in Different Types of Communication Systems

EMI has varying impacts across different types of communication systems. Some systems are more resilient to interference, while others require more sophisticated mitigation techniques.

1. **Cellular Networks**: Cellular systems operate across multiple frequency bands and use sophisticated methods like frequency division, time division, and code division to avoid interference. However, EMI can still lead to dropped calls, poor signal quality, or data corruption. For instance, interference from nearby devices such as wireless routers, Bluetooth devices, or even neighboring cell towers can cause signal degradation. To mitigate these issues, cellular networks employ advanced technologies such as frequency hopping and adaptive power control to minimize the impact of EMI.
2. **Wi-Fi Networks**: Wi-Fi systems operate in the 2.4 GHz and 5 GHz frequency bands, which are shared by a variety of devices, including microwaves, cordless phones, and baby monitors. These devices can cause EMI, resulting in slower data transfer rates or dropped connections in Wi-Fi networks. To reduce the impact of interference, Wi-Fi networks often switch channels or use advanced error-correction techniques, but performance may still suffer when the interference is severe.

3. **Radar Systems**: Radar systems rely on RF signals to detect objects and measure their distance and speed. EMI can cause radar systems to misinterpret signals, resulting in false detections, reduced accuracy, or missed targets. For example, in aviation, EMI from nearby communication systems or radar systems can interfere with an aircraft's radar, leading to inaccurate readings and potentially compromising flight safety. To mitigate this, radar systems often employ signal processing algorithms to filter out noise and enhance target detection.

4. **Satellite Communication**: Satellites communicate with ground stations and other satellites via RF signals, and EMI can significantly degrade these signals. Natural sources such as solar flares or cosmic radiation can disrupt satellite signals, while artificial sources like terrestrial jammers can completely block communication. The use of frequency allocation, directional antennas, and advanced modulation techniques helps minimize the effects of EMI in satellite communication, but these systems remain vulnerable to interference.

5. **Broadcast Television and Radio**: Broadcast systems use RF signals to transmit audio and video content over wide areas. EMI from various sources, including electrical equipment, wireless devices, and even weather phenomena, can disrupt these broadcasts. For example, interference can cause static in audio or pixelation in video, affecting the quality of the broadcast. Broadcasters use RF shielding, filters, and frequency coordination to mitigate EMI and maintain signal quality.

6. **GPS Systems**: GPS systems rely on precise timing and frequency to determine the location of a receiver. EMI can disrupt the reception of GPS signals, causing inaccuracies in location data. Urban environments with tall buildings or interference from nearby electronic devices are common sources of EMI in GPS systems. Anti-jamming technologies, such as adaptive filtering and signal processing, are used to enhance GPS system resilience against EMI.

Case Studies of EMI Disruption

1. **The 2003 Northeast Blackout**: One of the most notable real-world examples of EMI disrupting communication and electrical systems occurred during the 2003 Northeast blackout in the United States. A series of cascading power grid failures led to widespread communication failures in industrial control systems and electrical grids, partly caused by EMI from malfunctioning equipment. This incident highlighted the importance of EMI mitigation in critical infrastructure systems.

2. **2008 GPS Signal Interference**: In 2008, a military-grade jamming device caused interference with civilian GPS signals in parts of the United States. This disruption affected a variety of applications, including aviation, navigation, and vehicle tracking. The incident underscored the vulnerability of GPS systems to EMI and the potential consequences of unregulated jamming technology.

3. **Wi-Fi Interference in Hospitals**: In healthcare environments, EMI can severely affect communication between medical devices, such as patient monitors and infusion pumps. For example, in a case study at a large hospital, interference from nearby Wi-Fi routers caused false alarms in patient monitoring systems. The hospital had to implement stricter guidelines for Wi-Fi frequency management and RF shielding to ensure the reliability of medical equipment.

Conclusion

Electromagnetic Interference (EMI) has a significant impact on the performance of communication systems, from cellular networks and Wi-Fi to satellite communication and radar. The degradation of signal quality, dropped connections, data corruption, and reduced range are just a few of the issues caused by EMI. In highly sensitive environments like hospitals, aviation, and defense, the consequences of EMI can be severe and even life-threatening.

Mitigating EMI requires a combination of engineering solutions, such as RF shielding, filtering, and advanced signal processing, as well as regulatory measures to control and manage interference. As wireless communication systems become more complex and widely used, understanding the impact of EMI and developing effective strategies to combat it will be crucial for ensuring the reliability and security of these systems. In the following chapters, we will explore methods for mitigating EMI, including RF shielding, signal suppression, and the use of advanced technologies to protect communication systems from interference.

Chapter 5: Introduction to RF Shielding
What is RF Shielding?

Radio Frequency (RF) shielding is a protective barrier that is designed to prevent electromagnetic interference (EMI) from either entering or leaving a device or system. RF shielding is crucial for maintaining the integrity of communication systems by blocking unwanted RF signals that can cause disruptions or degrade performance. It works by absorbing, reflecting, or rerouting the electromagnetic waves that would otherwise interfere with the functioning of electronic equipment.

In simple terms, RF shielding is the process of enclosing sensitive electronic devices or systems in a material that blocks or reduces electromagnetic radiation. This can help prevent the external interference of signals from disrupting the device, while also ensuring that the device's signals do not leak and cause interference to other nearby systems.

RF shielding is essential in various industries, such as telecommunications, aerospace, military, and healthcare, where interference can lead to performance degradation, safety concerns, and security vulnerabilities. Whether it's a mobile phone, a medical device, or a military radar system, RF shielding plays a key role in ensuring reliable and secure operation.

Principles of RF Shielding and Its Importance in Protecting Sensitive Equipment

RF shielding operates based on several key principles:

1. **Reflection**: A material with high conductivity reflects the electromagnetic waves that impinge on it, redirecting them away from the shielded device. This is particularly important in systems where the incoming signal is unwanted and needs to be blocked.
2. **Absorption**: Shielding materials can also absorb incoming RF energy, converting it into heat. This principle is often used in combination with reflection to provide effective protection across a broader range of frequencies.
3. **Conduction**: A conductive shield works by rerouting the unwanted electromagnetic energy along the surface of the material. The conductivity of the material allows it to create a pathway for the electromagnetic waves to flow along the shield and away from the protected equipment.
4. **Skin Effect**: The skin effect refers to the tendency of alternating current (AC) to flow only on the surface of a conductor at higher frequencies. This is particularly relevant in RF shielding, as the shield material must be able to conduct electromagnetic waves at high frequencies effectively.

The importance of RF shielding lies in its ability to protect sensitive equipment from external sources of interference and prevent the equipment's emissions from contaminating the surrounding environment. This is crucial for:

- **Maintaining signal integrity**: Shielding ensures that communication systems, whether they are transmitting or receiving, remain free from unwanted signals, preserving the quality of data transmission.
- **Protecting critical equipment**: In industries such as healthcare, aerospace, and defense, maintaining the operation of critical systems is paramount. Shielding helps safeguard these systems from interference that could lead to malfunction or failure.
- **Meeting regulatory compliance**: Many industries are governed by regulations that require systems to be shielded to minimize EMI and ensure that they do not interfere with other devices or communication systems. RF shielding helps ensure compliance with these standards.

Materials Used for RF Shielding

The effectiveness of RF shielding depends largely on the material used. Different materials offer varying levels of shielding effectiveness depending on their electrical conductivity, magnetic permeability, and the thickness of the material. Some of the most commonly used materials for RF shielding include:

1. **Copper**: Copper is one of the most widely used materials for RF shielding due to its excellent electrical conductivity. It is highly effective at absorbing and reflecting electromagnetic waves, making it a popular choice for shielding in telecommunications, consumer electronics, and military applications. Copper's primary disadvantage is its cost and susceptibility to corrosion, which is often addressed by adding protective coatings.
2. **Aluminum**: Aluminum is another commonly used material for RF shielding. It is lightweight, highly conductive, and resistant to corrosion, making it ideal for many commercial and industrial applications. While not as effective as copper in terms of conductivity, aluminum is often used in aerospace, automotive, and consumer electronics for shielding purposes.
3. **Steel**: Steel, particularly stainless steel, is used for RF shielding in environments where higher durability and strength are required. Steel is often employed in military and industrial applications because it offers robust physical protection in addition to its electromagnetic shielding capabilities. However, steel is less effective than copper and aluminum in terms of conductivity.

4. **Nickel**: Nickel is used in specialized RF shielding applications where corrosion resistance is important, such as in marine environments. It is often used in combination with other metals, such as copper, to enhance the shielding effectiveness. Nickel-coated materials are often used in applications like medical devices and electronic enclosures.

5. **Conductive Plastics**: Conductive plastics are an emerging alternative to traditional metal shields. These materials are lightweight, flexible, and easy to shape, making them ideal for portable or custom devices. Conductive polymers, carbon composites, and other materials are used in applications such as wearable electronics and portable communication devices.

6. **Mesh Materials**: For specific applications, RF shielding can be achieved using mesh materials, where fine wires are woven into a mesh pattern. These meshes allow for airflow and visibility while still providing effective shielding. This type of shielding is commonly used in military equipment and secure communication enclosures, as it offers a balance between shielding and practical use.

Types of Shielding: Faraday Cages, Conductive Coatings, and Enclosures

There are several methods and structures used in RF shielding, each suited to different applications. The main types of shielding are:

1. **Faraday Cages**: A Faraday cage is an enclosure made of a conductive material that completely surrounds the equipment or area that needs to be shielded. The principle behind a Faraday cage is that the conductive material redistributes the electromagnetic waves that strike the cage, preventing them from penetrating the shielded space. Faraday cages are highly effective at blocking both external interference and preventing emissions from escaping the device. These are widely used in military, aerospace, and laboratory environments where precise and uninterrupted operation of sensitive equipment is required.
2. **Conductive Coatings**: Conductive coatings are applied to the surface of enclosures or components to provide RF shielding. These coatings typically consist of metallic particles suspended in a polymer or liquid, which can be sprayed or painted onto the surface of the item being shielded. Conductive coatings are ideal for situations where it is impractical to use solid metal enclosures, such as on electronic circuit boards, housing for consumer electronics, or medical devices. While they may not offer as high a level of shielding as solid metal enclosures, conductive coatings can be a cost-effective and versatile solution.

3. **Enclosures and Boxes**: For many devices, simple metal enclosures or boxes provide sufficient RF shielding. These enclosures are typically made from materials such as aluminum or stainless steel and are designed to completely surround and protect the device from external electromagnetic interference. These enclosures are commonly used in communication devices, electronics, and instrumentation, where physical protection is just as important as electromagnetic shielding.

4. **Gaskets and Seals**: In many cases, RF shielding is applied not just to the outer casing of a device but also to the gaps and seams where electromagnetic waves could leak through. Gaskets and seals made of conductive rubber, metal foils, or meshes are used to close gaps around doors, panels, and connectors in enclosures. These seals are crucial for maintaining the integrity of the shielding and preventing leakage of electromagnetic radiation.

Conclusion

RF shielding is a critical technology for protecting sensitive electronic equipment from electromagnetic interference (EMI) and preventing the unwanted emission of RF signals. Through various materials and shielding structures, RF shielding helps ensure the reliable operation of communication systems, medical devices, military equipment, and other critical technologies. By using materials such as copper, aluminum, and steel, and employing shielding techniques like Faraday cages and conductive coatings, effective shielding solutions can be implemented for a wide range of applications.

As the demand for RF-sensitive devices grows, especially with the advent of IoT, 5G networks, and complex communication systems, the importance of effective RF shielding will only increase. In the following chapters, we will explore how RF shielding works in practice, the materials and technologies behind it, and how to design products to minimize EMI, ensuring optimal performance in the face of interference challenges.

Chapter 6: Principles of Signal Suppression

Signal suppression refers to the techniques used to reduce or eliminate unwanted signals in a communication system, especially in environments where electromagnetic interference (EMI) or RF jamming may degrade system performance. Whether dealing with noise, spurious signals, or intentional jamming, signal suppression is essential for maintaining the integrity and quality of communication.

In this chapter, we will explore the various methods of signal suppression, including active and passive techniques, and discuss the types of devices and systems used to mitigate unwanted signals both during transmission and reception.

Techniques for Signal Suppression: Active and Passive Methods

Signal suppression can be achieved using either passive or active methods, depending on the nature of the interference and the specific system requirements.

Passive Methods

- **Attenuators**: An attenuator is a device used to reduce the amplitude of a signal, effectively lowering its strength. It is a passive component that does not introduce any distortion, and it is commonly used in RF systems to decrease the strength of unwanted signals. Attenuators are used in a variety of applications, including power amplifiers, signal routing, and testing systems.
- **Filters**: Filters are electronic circuits or components that allow signals of certain frequencies to pass through while blocking or attenuating others. The primary function of a filter is to isolate desired signals from unwanted interference. Filters can be designed to target specific frequency bands (such as low-pass, high-pass, band-pass, or band-stop filters) to either suppress high-frequency noise or allow the signal of interest to pass without interference.
- **Shielding**: Shielding, discussed in the previous chapter, is a passive method of signal suppression. It involves using conductive materials to block external electromagnetic fields from entering or leaving a device. By preventing unwanted RF signals from reaching sensitive components, shielding acts as a protective barrier against both EMI and intentional jamming.

- **Grounding**: Proper grounding techniques are essential to reduce EMI by providing a low-resistance path for electrical signals to flow safely into the earth. Grounding helps dissipate unwanted electromagnetic energy and prevents it from affecting sensitive equipment. It is especially important in high-frequency communication systems where signal quality is critical.

Active Methods

- **Active Noise Cancellation (ANC)**: ANC is a technique where an "anti-noise" signal is generated to cancel out unwanted noise. This is typically achieved by producing a signal with the same amplitude but an inverted phase, which effectively nullifies the original interference. ANC systems are used in applications such as audio systems and communications to minimize background noise and improve signal quality.
- **Adaptive Filtering**: Adaptive filtering is a dynamic method of signal suppression that adjusts its parameters in real-time to effectively counteract interference. Adaptive filters continuously measure the interference characteristics and modify their behavior to cancel or suppress unwanted signals. These filters are particularly useful in environments with varying interference levels or where the interference source changes over time.
- **Digital Signal Processing (DSP)**: DSP involves using algorithms to modify or filter signals in the digital domain. Signal processing techniques can be used to filter out noise, reduce distortion, and remove unwanted components from received signals. In systems affected by RF jamming, DSP can identify and suppress interfering signals in real-time, significantly improving the quality of the received signal.

- **Jamming Countermeasures**: In the case of RF jamming, active countermeasures can be deployed to counteract intentional interference. These measures may include techniques such as frequency hopping, spread spectrum communication, or even the use of jammers that emit signals on the same frequency as the jammer in an attempt to overpower the interference. These active methods help restore communication by preventing the jammer from disrupting the system entirely.

Filters, Attenuators, and Other Suppression Devices

A wide range of devices can be employed to suppress unwanted signals, each tailored to specific types of interference or communication systems.

1. **Band-Pass Filters**: Band-pass filters are used to allow signals within a specific frequency range to pass while blocking frequencies outside of that range. These filters are especially useful in systems where only a narrow frequency band is relevant, such as in Wi-Fi, cellular communications, or radar systems. Band-pass filters can be used to suppress unwanted signals that fall outside the desired communication frequency.

2. **Low-Pass and High-Pass Filters**: Low-pass filters allow low-frequency signals to pass while attenuating higher frequencies, and high-pass filters do the opposite by blocking lower frequencies while allowing higher frequencies to pass. These filters are often used in audio systems, power supplies, and RF circuits to remove noise or unwanted signals.

3. **Notch Filters**: Notch filters, also known as band-stop filters, are used to attenuate a very specific frequency or narrow band of frequencies. These filters are ideal for isolating a particular source of interference, such as a harmonic distortion or a spurious signal that might be affecting the system.

4. **Ferrite Beads**: Ferrite beads are passive components used to suppress high-frequency noise in signal and power lines. They work by converting high-frequency electromagnetic energy into heat, thus reducing the amount of interference that reaches sensitive components. Ferrite beads are commonly used in cables and power supply lines in consumer electronics and industrial systems.

5. **Attenuators**: Attenuators reduce the power of the signal before it reaches the receiver. They are essential for managing signal levels, preventing overloading of sensitive components, and mitigating the effects of signal reflections or unwanted interference. Attenuators are widely used in RF systems where the signal strength needs to be controlled to maintain signal integrity.

Methods for Mitigating Unwanted Signals in Both Transmit and Receive Modes

The suppression of unwanted signals is crucial not only for improving the reception of signals but also for preventing unwanted emissions during transmission. Here's how signal suppression is applied to both transmit and receive modes:

Transmit Mode Suppression

- **Power Amplifier Linearization**: Power amplifiers are critical components in communication systems, and their non-linear behavior can lead to signal distortion and the generation of harmonic distortion. Techniques such as predistortion or feedback linearization are used to reduce these effects and maintain signal quality.
- **Pre-Transmission Filtering**: Filters can be installed before the transmission circuitry to ensure that only the desired frequencies are transmitted. These filters prevent unwanted sidebands or harmonic distortions from being emitted, thus ensuring that the signal does not interfere with other systems or violate regulatory requirements.
- **Transmit Beamforming**: Beamforming is a technique where the transmission of signals is directed in a specific direction using phased array antennas. This helps reduce the power of the signal in other directions, thereby reducing the potential for interference with nearby systems.

Receive Mode Suppression

- **Pre-Reception Filtering**: Filters can be used at the input of the receiver to block out-of-band interference, ensuring that only the desired signal is passed to the receiver. This is especially important in systems like radar, satellite communications, and wireless systems where multiple frequencies may be in use.
- **Low-Noise Amplifiers (LNAs)**: LNAs are used to amplify weak signals while minimizing noise amplification. LNAs are essential for improving the sensitivity of communication systems, ensuring that the receiver can detect low-level signals while rejecting interference.
- **Adaptive Reception Techniques**: Similar to adaptive filtering, adaptive reception techniques dynamically adjust the receiver's sensitivity or frequency response to optimize signal quality. These techniques are especially useful in environments with fluctuating levels of interference, such as urban areas with heavy RF traffic.

Conclusion

Signal suppression is a vital aspect of maintaining the integrity and quality of communication systems in environments affected by RF jamming or electromagnetic interference (EMI). By employing both active and passive suppression methods, including filters, attenuators, and advanced techniques like adaptive filtering and noise cancellation, systems can mitigate the effects of unwanted signals in both transmission and reception modes.

As RF and communication technologies continue to evolve, the development of more sophisticated suppression techniques, such as digital signal processing (DSP) and adaptive systems, will further enhance the resilience of these systems against interference. In the next chapters, we will explore how signal suppression techniques work in conjunction with other technologies, such as RF shielding and jamming countermeasures, to provide comprehensive protection for communication systems.

Chapter 7: RF Jamming Techniques

RF jamming is a critical tool in both military and civil applications, serving to disrupt, degrade, or deny the functionality of communication systems by overwhelming their signals with interference. In this chapter, we explore the different RF jamming techniques used to block or degrade communication systems, from basic methods to more advanced strategies. We will also examine the technologies behind jamming devices, the countermeasures that can be employed, and the legal and ethical considerations involved in the use of RF jamming.

Various Methods of RF Jamming

RF jamming can be classified into several types based on the signal characteristics and how the jamming signal is applied. The most common techniques include noise jamming, deceptive jamming, spot jamming, and sweep jamming. Each has its own applications and effectiveness in different scenarios.

1. **Noise Jamming**: Noise jamming involves broadcasting random or continuous interference signals over the same frequency band as the target communication system. This type of jamming essentially "drowns out" the desired signal with noise, making it difficult for receivers to distinguish the legitimate signal from the noise. The effectiveness of noise jamming depends on the power of the jamming signal and the signal-to-noise ratio (SNR) of the target system. Noise jamming can be either narrowband, affecting a specific frequency, or broadband, affecting a wide range of frequencies.

2. **Deceptive Jamming**: Deceptive jamming involves injecting misleading or false signals into the communication channel. Rather than simply overpowering the target signal with noise, deceptive jamming manipulates the target receiver's interpretation of the data. For example, in radar systems, deceptive jamming can create false returns or fake signals, leading to inaccurate readings or incorrect information being processed. In cellular communication, deceptive jamming may involve sending fabricated data or control messages to confuse the system.

3. **Spot Jamming**: Spot jamming is a more focused form of interference, targeting a narrow frequency band to jam a specific communication signal. This technique can be highly effective when the target system uses a fixed frequency or a small set of frequencies. Spot jammers are typically designed to provide high power on the selected frequency, thus minimizing the impact on other communication systems. Spot jamming is commonly used in military and law enforcement applications to disable specific communications or to prevent specific signals from reaching their destination.
4. **Sweep Jamming**: Sweep jamming, also called frequency-hopping jamming, involves shifting the jamming signal across different frequencies in a rapid manner to block or confuse frequency-hopping systems. Sweep jammers are designed to target systems that use frequency-hopping spread spectrum (FHSS), which rapidly switches between frequencies to avoid interference. Sweep jamming can disrupt the ability of such systems to maintain synchronization, rendering the communication channel unusable.

5. **Barrage Jamming**: Barrage jamming is a method of flooding a wide frequency range with interference. This is often used in scenarios where multiple signals need to be disrupted across a broad spectrum. Barrage jamming is typically less effective than narrowband jamming but is used in situations where broad disruption is needed, such as during an electronic warfare campaign or in areas where many different communication channels are in use.

6. **Spoofing (False Jamming)**: Spoofing is a form of deceptive jamming where the attacker sends out a false signal that mimics the target communication signal. In the context of GPS systems, for instance, spoofing involves transmitting fake satellite signals that mislead GPS receivers into calculating incorrect positions. This form of jamming is particularly dangerous as it does not only disrupt the signal but also provides incorrect data, potentially leading to critical system errors.

Advanced Jamming Technologies

In addition to traditional jamming methods, advancements in digital signal processing (DSP) and spread spectrum technology have enabled the development of more sophisticated and adaptive jamming techniques.

1. **Digital Signal Processing (DSP) Jamming**: Digital signal processing allows for the creation of more complex and adaptive jamming signals. DSP-based jammers are capable of analyzing the target signal in real-time and adjusting the jamming parameters to match the characteristics of the target communication system. These jammers can generate highly effective interference by exploiting vulnerabilities in the target signal's modulation scheme, frequency band, or coding method. DSP jamming is increasingly used in modern electronic warfare and cyber-attack scenarios.
2. **Spread Spectrum Jamming**: Spread spectrum jamming involves targeting signals that use spread spectrum modulation techniques (such as frequency hopping or direct-sequence spread spectrum). By spreading the jamming signal over a wide range of frequencies, this method can disrupt communication systems that rely on spread spectrum technology. One of the advantages of spread spectrum jamming is its ability to interfere with multiple channels simultaneously, making it a powerful tool for disabling wide-area communication networks.

3. **Smart Jammers**: Smart jammers use artificial intelligence (AI) or machine learning algorithms to adapt to changing environments and optimize their interference strategy. These jammers can detect and identify the specific characteristics of the target communication system and dynamically adjust their jamming techniques to improve effectiveness. For example, smart jammers can focus their energy on the most vulnerable parts of a communication system, such as weak signal areas or certain frequencies, without causing unnecessary disruption to other systems.

4. **Phased Array Jamming**: Phased array antennas are often used in radar and communication systems for beamforming and directional transmission. Phased array jammers exploit these antennas by creating an interference pattern that matches the beam direction, allowing them to effectively block or degrade the performance of specific radar or communication signals. These jammers can also adjust their direction to track and target moving systems, making them highly effective in dynamic environments.

Countermeasures and Tactics Used Against Jamming

To protect against RF jamming, communication systems and defense technologies employ a variety of countermeasures and tactics. These techniques are designed to ensure that communications remain secure and effective even in the presence of intentional interference.

1. **Frequency Hopping**: Frequency hopping is one of the most common countermeasures used to defend against narrowband and spot jamming. In frequency hopping, the transmitter and receiver rapidly change their operating frequencies according to a predefined sequence. This makes it much harder for a jammer to target the communication signal effectively since the frequency changes continuously, often at a rate faster than the jammer can keep up with.

2. **Spread Spectrum Techniques**: Spread spectrum techniques, including direct-sequence spread spectrum (DSSS) and frequency hopping spread spectrum (FHSS), spread the signal over a wide bandwidth. This reduces the impact of jamming by making it harder for the jammer to focus on the desired signal. Spread spectrum communication is more resistant to interference because the signal is more dispersed, making it less likely to be completely overwhelmed by external noise or jamming signals.

3. **Adaptive Power Control**: Adaptive power control adjusts the power level of the transmitter to maintain the strength of the communication signal above the level of interference. This is especially important in wireless networks and satellite communications, where environmental factors can cause signal degradation. By dynamically adjusting transmission power, the system can ensure a strong signal even in the presence of jamming or interference.

4. **Directional Antennas**: Directional antennas are used to focus the communication signal in a specific direction, reducing the potential for interference from unwanted sources. By using beamforming technology, the antenna can direct the signal toward the receiver while minimizing the amount of energy directed toward potential jammers. This helps improve the overall signal-to-noise ratio and makes it more difficult for jammers to intercept or block the signal.

5. **Encryption**: In addition to physical and technical countermeasures, encryption is a critical defense against jamming, particularly in military and secure communication systems. By encrypting the signal, even if the jammer is able to interfere with or block the signal, it is difficult for the jamming system to decode or alter the transmitted data.

Legal and Ethical Implications of RF Jamming

The use of RF jamming, especially in civilian applications, is highly regulated due to its potential to cause widespread disruption. Jamming signals can interfere with essential communication systems, including emergency services, aviation, and communication networks, leading to significant legal and ethical concerns.

- **Legality**: In many countries, such as the United States, the use of jamming devices is illegal unless authorized by government agencies for specific purposes, such as national defense or law enforcement. The Federal Communications Commission (FCC) in the U.S. strictly prohibits the use of jammers in public or commercial sectors, and violators can face heavy fines and imprisonment.
- **Ethical Considerations**: Jamming technology can be used for malicious purposes, such as disrupting public services or interfering with personal communication. In civilian contexts, the use of jamming is considered unethical due to the potential harm it can cause, including preventing people from accessing critical services. On the other hand, jamming technology is seen as a legitimate tool in military operations, where it is used to deny adversaries the ability to communicate or use radar.

Conclusion

RF jamming techniques play a critical role in disrupting communication systems, both in military and civilian applications. From basic noise jamming to sophisticated digital signal processing, the methods of jamming continue to evolve as technology advances. Countermeasures such as frequency hopping, spread spectrum techniques, and encryption help mitigate the impact of jamming, ensuring that systems remain functional even in challenging environments.

As RF jamming becomes increasingly advanced, understanding its principles and countermeasures is essential for building resilient communication systems. The legal and ethical issues surrounding jamming also highlight the need for careful regulation and responsible use of this technology to prevent misuse and unintended consequences.

Chapter 8: Electromagnetic Compatibility (EMC)//
Introduction to EMC and Why It's Important in Modern Devices

Electromagnetic Compatibility (EMC) refers to the ability of electrical and electronic devices to function as intended in their electromagnetic environment, without causing interference to other devices and without being susceptible to interference from other sources. EMC is a critical consideration in the design and operation of modern communication systems, consumer electronics, medical devices, automotive systems, and industrial equipment.

In an increasingly interconnected world, electronic devices rely on shared electromagnetic spectra to transmit data, control signals, and power various systems. As the number of electronic devices increases, so does the potential for interference, which can lead to system malfunctions, reduced performance, or even catastrophic failures. EMC ensures that these devices coexist harmoniously by minimizing electromagnetic interference (EMI) and ensuring that devices are adequately shielded from external noise.

EMC is especially important in high-speed communication systems, medical equipment, and military or aerospace technologies where the consequences of failure can be critical. Proper EMC management helps maintain reliability, functionality, and safety in these complex systems, which is why manufacturers must adhere to rigorous standards and guidelines during design and testing.

Testing and Measuring EMC

EMC testing is the process of evaluating whether a device or system meets the required electromagnetic compatibility standards. This is done by assessing both the electromagnetic emissions (the energy a device emits) and its susceptibility to external electromagnetic interference. EMC testing helps ensure that devices will not interfere with each other or become impaired by external interference in real-world environments.

There are several testing methods used to measure EMC:

1. **Radiated Emissions Testing**: This test measures the amount of electromagnetic energy emitted by a device into the surrounding space. Devices that emit high levels of radiation may interfere with nearby equipment. Radiated emissions testing is usually performed in an anechoic chamber to isolate the device from external signals and accurately measure its emissions. The emissions are often measured in frequency ranges (e.g., from 30 MHz to 1 GHz) to ensure that they stay within permissible limits.

2. **Conducted Emissions Testing**: Conducted emissions testing assesses the electromagnetic noise that travels along the power supply lines (e.g., via power cords or cables). This is important because EMI can enter or exit a device through its power connection. The device is tested to ensure it doesn't inject harmful noise into the electrical grid or become affected by disturbances in the power line.

3. **Electromagnetic Susceptibility (EMS) Testing**: EMS testing determines how well a device can withstand external electromagnetic fields without malfunctioning. The device is exposed to controlled levels of interference in a test environment, and the impact on its performance is observed. This helps ensure that the device can continue operating reliably in environments with natural or artificial electromagnetic disturbances, such as in factories, vehicles, or urban areas with high RF traffic.

4. **Electrostatic Discharge (ESD) Testing**: ESD testing evaluates a device's ability to withstand sudden electrostatic discharges, which can be generated by contact with human operators or other objects. This is particularly important for devices with sensitive components, such as semiconductors, which can easily be damaged by even small electrostatic charges.

5. **Immunity Testing**: Immunity testing examines a device's ability to function properly in the presence of external electromagnetic interference. This includes testing the device against both continuous signals (like those generated by radio transmitters) and transient disturbances (such as lightning-induced surges). The goal is to ensure that the device operates normally despite exposure to common electromagnetic disturbances.

Designing Systems for EMC Compliance

Designing systems to meet EMC standards requires careful planning and the implementation of various strategies to reduce electromagnetic interference and ensure system immunity. Effective EMC design begins in the early stages of product development and involves addressing potential sources of EMI and identifying ways to mitigate them.

Key considerations in designing for EMC compliance include:

1. **Component Selection**: Choosing components that meet EMC specifications is essential. These include choosing low-emission components, selecting parts that are robust to EMI, and ensuring that all components are properly grounded and shielded. For example, low-noise power supplies, well-designed integrated circuits (ICs), and EMI-resistant connectors help minimize unwanted interference.

2. **Grounding and Shielding**: Proper grounding and shielding techniques are crucial in minimizing EMI. A well-designed grounding system helps to safely dissipate any unwanted electrical energy. Shielding materials, such as copper or aluminum, can be used to create protective barriers around sensitive equipment to prevent EMI from entering or exiting. This could involve shielding the entire device or focusing on specific components that are more vulnerable to interference.

3. **PCB Layout and Design**: In designing printed circuit boards (PCBs) for EMC compliance, careful layout is key. Signal traces should be kept as short as possible, and sensitive components should be placed away from high-frequency noise sources. Ground planes and shielding can help reduce the risk of EMI by isolating circuits and preventing cross-talk between traces. The design should also minimize the use of components that generate high-frequency noise.

4. **Filtering**: Filters are used to block unwanted high-frequency signals while allowing desired signals to pass through. Filters can be used at various points in a circuit, including the input and output ports, as well as power supply lines. For example, low-pass filters allow low-frequency signals to pass while filtering out high-frequency noise, making them a common component in EMI control.

5. **Cabling and Connectors**: The type of cables and connectors used can significantly impact EMC. Shielded cables are often used to prevent EMI from traveling along the wires, while properly designed connectors ensure that the shield remains intact and that electromagnetic leakage is minimized. Additionally, twisted pair cables can be used to cancel out induced noise in data lines.

6. **Reducing Electromagnetic Emissions**: Careful attention must be paid to the emission characteristics of a device. This may involve designing the device with lower emission levels, minimizing the number of cables and connectors that radiate signals, and using conductive enclosures to contain emissions. A device's emission characteristics can also be reduced by using low-power transmission systems or reducing the clock speeds in digital systems.

7. **Regulatory Compliance**: Manufacturers must design their systems to comply with regional and international EMC standards and regulations. These standards ensure that electronic devices do not cause harmful interference to other equipment and are resilient to external disturbances. Some of the most widely recognized regulatory standards include:

- **FCC Part 15** (U.S. Federal Communications Commission regulations)
- **EN 55022** (European standard for limits and methods of measurement of radio disturbance)
- **CISPR 11** (International standard for industrial, scientific, and medical equipment emissions)

Best Practices for Minimizing EMI in Product Development

Ensuring that a product meets EMC standards requires the integration of best practices throughout the development cycle, from design through testing and certification. Some best practices include:

1. **Early EMC Consideration**: Begin considering EMC requirements early in the design process. This involves identifying potential sources of EMI, selecting appropriate components, and planning how to manage shielding, grounding, and filtering.

2. **Prototyping and Testing**: Prototype the design and perform EMC testing at each stage of development to identify potential issues early. Use both pre-compliance testing and formal compliance testing to ensure the device will meet the required standards. Testing during development can help identify problems before manufacturing and reduce the likelihood of costly redesigns.

3. **Iterative Design and Improvement**: EMC issues may not be fully addressed in the first iteration of a design, so an iterative process is often necessary. Continuously test the product under real-world electromagnetic conditions and improve the design to achieve better performance.

4. **Use of Simulation Software**: Simulation software can be a powerful tool for predicting and analyzing EMC behavior in designs. Tools like electromagnetic field solvers, circuit simulators, and PCB layout software can help engineers visualize how electromagnetic waves will behave in a device and identify potential areas for improvement.

Conclusion

Electromagnetic Compatibility (EMC) is a crucial aspect of modern device design, ensuring that systems operate reliably and do not interfere with each other. Understanding and applying EMC principles during the design process can significantly reduce the risk of EMI and help ensure that devices meet regulatory standards for both emissions and immunity.

By carefully considering grounding, shielding, layout, and filtering techniques, engineers can build devices that are resilient to external interference while minimizing their own electromagnetic emissions. Through continuous testing, iteration, and use of modern design tools, manufacturers can create systems that meet the increasingly stringent EMC requirements of today's electromagnetic landscape.

In the next chapters, we will explore practical strategies for mitigating EMI in various systems and discuss emerging technologies that are shaping the future of electromagnetic protection and control.

Chapter 9: EMI Mitigation Techniques

Electromagnetic Interference (EMI) is an ever-present challenge in the design and operation of modern electronic devices. Whether in consumer electronics, industrial systems, or mission-critical communication networks, EMI can cause disruptions that affect system performance and reliability. As such, understanding and implementing effective EMI mitigation techniques is essential for ensuring that devices meet the required electromagnetic compatibility (EMC) standards.

This chapter explores the various strategies and techniques used to mitigate EMI, including shielding, grounding, and filtering. We will also discuss the importance of good design practices and real-world examples of successful EMI mitigation in both commercial and industrial systems.

Shielding, Grounding, and Filtering for EMI Control

Three of the most critical methods for controlling EMI are **shielding**, **grounding**, and **filtering**. These techniques are used to either prevent EMI from affecting sensitive components, reduce the emissions of unwanted interference, or minimize the impact of external disturbances on devices and systems.

Shielding

- **Enclosures**: Devices and systems are often housed within enclosures made from conductive materials (e.g., aluminum, copper) to prevent EMI from entering or leaving the device. These enclosures are commonly used in consumer electronics, medical devices, and industrial control systems.
- **Faraday Cages**: A Faraday cage is a complete enclosure that blocks external static and non-static electric fields. It is designed to completely surround a device with a conductive material to protect it from both radiated and conducted EMI. Faraday cages are often used in highly sensitive systems like data centers, research laboratories, and military equipment.
- **Conductive Coatings**: Conductive coatings, typically made of carbon or metallic particles embedded in a polymer, can be applied to circuit boards, cables, and enclosures to provide EMI shielding. These coatings are an effective solution for applications where traditional metal shielding would be too bulky or impractical.

Grounding

- **Single-Point Grounding**: A single-point grounding system ensures that all components within a system are connected to a single grounding point. This minimizes the possibility of creating unwanted ground loops, which can act as antennas and radiate EMI.
- **Chassis Grounding**: Devices with metal casings often rely on chassis grounding, where the metal casing itself is grounded to dissipate any electromagnetic energy that may accumulate on the device.
- **Power Grounding**: Proper grounding of power supplies is critical to prevent EMI from entering the system through the power lines. Power conditioning systems often include filters, surge protectors, and other components to ensure a clean and stable power source that doesn't contribute to EMI.

Filtering

- **Low-Pass Filters**: These filters allow low-frequency signals to pass through while blocking higher frequencies. Low-pass filters are commonly used in power supply lines to prevent high-frequency noise from entering sensitive circuits.
- **High-Pass Filters**: High-pass filters, on the other hand, allow higher frequencies to pass while blocking low frequencies. These are often used to eliminate low-frequency noise or power hum from the system.
- **Band-Pass Filters**: Band-pass filters are used when a specific frequency range must be isolated, either to allow only a narrow range of signals through or to block interference within a particular frequency band.
- **Notch Filters**: Notch filters are designed to block a very specific frequency or narrow band of frequencies. These are especially useful when dealing with known sources of interference, such as harmonic distortions or interference from nearby wireless devices.

Layout and Design Considerations for EMI Reduction in Circuits

Effective circuit design is crucial to minimize EMI and ensure that the system remains stable and reliable. The following layout and design strategies can significantly reduce EMI:

1. **Short Traces and Low-Impedance Paths**: Minimizing the length of signal traces and ensuring low-impedance paths helps reduce the generation of electromagnetic fields. Long traces can act as antennas, radiating unwanted EMI. By keeping traces as short as possible and routing them in a way that minimizes the loop area, designers can reduce the amount of radiation and interference.

2. **Differential Signal Lines**: Differential signaling, in which two complementary signals are transmitted on separate wires, is often used in high-speed communication systems (e.g., Ethernet, USB). Differential signals are less susceptible to noise because the noise that is picked up by the signal wires affects both signals equally, allowing the receiver to cancel out the noise.

3. **Use of Ground Planes**: Ground planes are continuous copper layers that provide a low-impedance path for returning current. Ground planes reduce noise and help to provide a stable reference voltage for circuits, particularly in high-speed systems. A well-designed ground plane can help control the return path for signals and prevent EMI from radiating from the system.

4. **Decoupling Capacitors**: Decoupling capacitors are used to smooth out power supply fluctuations and reduce noise that may be introduced by the power lines. These capacitors act as filters, bypassing high-frequency noise to ground, and are particularly important in digital circuits that experience fast switching and high-frequency noise.

5. **Component Placement**: Placing high-speed components (such as processors or RF modules) far from sensitive analog circuits helps prevent EMI from coupling into the system. Similarly, placing power supplies or high-frequency signals away from low-frequency circuits minimizes the potential for interference.

Power Line Conditioning and Electromagnetic Pulse (EMP) Protection

1. **Power Line Conditioning**: Power line conditioning is the process of ensuring that the electrical power entering a device is clean and free from disturbances. This is accomplished using various components such as surge protectors, line filters, and voltage regulators. Power line conditioning ensures that EMI from the power grid does not affect the operation of sensitive equipment.

2. **Electromagnetic Pulse (EMP) Protection**: Electromagnetic pulses are high-intensity bursts of electromagnetic radiation, often caused by nuclear explosions or lightning strikes. EMPs can severely disrupt electronic systems and cause permanent damage. To protect against EMPs, systems are often shielded using Faraday cages, and sensitive equipment may be fitted with surge protectors, filters, and other EMP-mitigation devices.

Real-World Examples of Effective EMI Mitigation Strategies

1. **Medical Devices**: Medical devices such as pacemakers and MRI machines are highly sensitive to EMI. To ensure their reliable operation, these devices are often shielded within metal enclosures and are designed to meet strict EMC standards. Filtering is also used to protect power lines and data connections from interference, ensuring that the device operates without being affected by nearby electronics.

2. **Automotive Systems**: Modern vehicles rely heavily on electronic control systems for everything from engine management to autonomous driving features. EMI from motors, power systems, and nearby electronics can disrupt these systems, leading to malfunctions. Automotive manufacturers implement shielding and grounding techniques, along with proper PCB layout design, to minimize EMI and ensure the vehicle's systems remain reliable.

3. **Aerospace Applications**: In aerospace, where communication systems are critical, EMI can interfere with navigation, radar, and other safety systems. Aircraft are designed with extensive shielding, and sensitive equipment is isolated within Faraday cages. Additionally, complex grounding systems are employed to prevent EMI from affecting avionics or other critical systems.

Conclusion

Effective EMI mitigation requires a multi-faceted approach that combines shielding, grounding, filtering, and thoughtful circuit design. Each component of the system must be designed to minimize both emissions and susceptibility to external interference. By incorporating best practices throughout the design and development process, manufacturers can create devices that operate reliably and comply with EMC standards, ensuring minimal disruption and maximum performance.

As electromagnetic environments become increasingly complex with the rise of 5G, IoT, and advanced communication systems, the importance of robust EMI mitigation strategies will continue to grow. In the next chapters, we will delve deeper into specific materials and technologies for RF shielding and explore advanced signal suppression techniques that complement these foundational methods.

Chapter 10: RF Shielding Materials and Technologies

In the world of electromagnetic protection and control, RF shielding plays a crucial role in ensuring the proper functioning of communication systems, consumer electronics, and other critical devices that are susceptible to interference. The key to effective RF shielding lies in the materials used, which must be selected based on their ability to block or attenuate unwanted electromagnetic waves. This chapter explores the various conductive materials used for RF shielding, compares their properties, and looks at emerging hybrid shielding methods and future trends in shielding materials.

Conductive Materials Used for RF Shielding

The choice of shielding material depends on factors such as the frequency of interference, the physical characteristics of the system, cost, and the environment in which the device will operate. Below are some of the most commonly used conductive materials for RF shielding:

Copper

Advantages

- Excellent conductivity.
- Highly effective at blocking high-frequency interference.
- Widely available and easy to work with.

Disadvantages

- Expensive compared to other materials.
- Prone to corrosion without protective coatings.

Aluminum

Advantages

- Cost-effective.
- Lightweight and resistant to corrosion.
- Easy to fabricate and form.

Disadvantages

- Lower conductivity than copper.
- Less effective at shielding very high-frequency signals.

Steel (Stainless Steel)

Advantages

- Strong and durable.
- Resistant to corrosion and high temperatures.
- Effective in a wide range of electromagnetic frequencies.

Disadvantages

- Heavier and less malleable than aluminum or copper.
- Higher cost than aluminum.

Nickel

Advantages

- Highly resistant to corrosion.
- Suitable for harsh environmental conditions.

Disadvantages

- Less conductive than copper and aluminum.
- More expensive than other shielding materials.

Carbon Composites

Advantages

- Lightweight and flexible.
- Can be incorporated into thin and wearable electronics.
- Conductivity can be tailored by adjusting the material composition.

Disadvantages

- May not provide as high shielding efficiency as metals.
- Expensive and still emerging in some applications.

Conductive Plastics

Advantages

- Lightweight and easy to mold.
- Versatile and can be used in a wide range of applications.
- Cost-effective compared to metals.

Disadvantages

- Lower conductivity than metals.
- May not provide as strong shielding effectiveness as metallic materials.

Comparison of Materials: Copper, Aluminum, Carbon Composites, etc.

When choosing a material for RF shielding, it's essential to weigh the trade-offs between performance, cost, weight, and durability. Here is a comparison of some of the most commonly used RF shielding materials:

Material	Conductivity	Cost	Durability	Weight	Common Applications
Copper	Excellent	High	Moderate	Heavy	High-performance electronics, aerospace, medical devices
Aluminum	Good	Low	Moderate	Light	Consumer electronics, automotive systems, communication equipment
Stainless Steel	Good	High	Excellent	Heavy	Military equipment, industrial systems, aviation
Nickel	Moderate	High	Excellent	Moderate	Marine environments, aerospace
Carbon Composites	Moderate	High	Moderate	Light	Wearable electronics, lightweight applications
Conductive Plastics	Low	Low	Moderate	Light	Consumer products, custom enclosures

Hybrid Shielding Methods (Metallic and Non-Metallic)

Hybrid shielding methods combine both metallic and non-metallic materials to optimize performance while minimizing cost and weight. For example, a shielding system might use a metal enclosure for high-frequency blocking and incorporate a conductive plastic coating for structural flexibility or additional EMI attenuation.

Some common hybrid shielding approaches include:

- **Metal Mesh Overlays**: A mesh of copper or aluminum is often applied to non-metallic enclosures, providing effective shielding without adding significant weight. This method is used in a variety of consumer electronics, including laptops and mobile phones.
- **Conductive Polymers with Metal Layers**: Metal layers can be bonded to the surface of conductive polymers to enhance shielding without increasing the material's weight. These hybrid materials are ideal for flexible electronics, such as smart clothing or flexible medical devices.

Future Trends in Shielding Materials

As technology advances, there is a growing demand for materials that offer better shielding efficiency, lighter weight, and more flexibility. Some of the emerging trends in shielding materials include:

1. **Graphene-based Materials**: Graphene, a single layer of carbon atoms arranged in a two-dimensional lattice, is a highly conductive material that shows great promise for future RF shielding applications. Its flexibility, high conductivity, and lightweight properties make it ideal for use in wearable electronics, flexible displays, and high-performance communication devices.
2. **Nanomaterials**: Nanotechnology is enabling the development of materials that can manipulate electromagnetic waves at the molecular level. These materials could provide unprecedented shielding efficiency in smaller, lighter forms, which would be beneficial in miniature devices and next-generation communication systems.
3. **Smart Shielding**: The development of "smart" materials, which can adapt to changing electromagnetic environments, is an exciting prospect for the future of RF shielding. These materials can dynamically alter their shielding properties in response to external interference, improving both their efficiency and effectiveness. For example, self-adjusting shielding systems might automatically change their conductivity or permeability depending on the level of EMI in the environment.

4. **Biodegradable Shielding Materials**: As sustainability becomes an increasing concern in the electronics industry, researchers are exploring biodegradable materials for RF shielding. These materials would provide temporary shielding during use but break down without harming the environment, offering a greener alternative to traditional metals and plastics.

Conclusion

RF shielding is an essential aspect of modern electromagnetic protection and control, and the choice of shielding material is critical in ensuring that devices function as intended. Copper, aluminum, and stainless steel have long been staples of RF shielding, while newer materials like carbon composites, conductive plastics, and graphene show promising potential for future applications. Hybrid shielding methods, which combine metallic and non-metallic materials, are becoming more popular for optimizing performance across different frequencies and environments.

As technology evolves, so too will the materials and methods used in RF shielding, with innovations in nanomaterials, smart shielding, and biodegradable options paving the way for more efficient and sustainable solutions. In the next chapters, we will explore how these materials and technologies can be integrated into product design and the role they play in ensuring electromagnetic compatibility (EMC) in modern systems.

Chapter 11: Designing for RF Shielding and EMI Control

Effective design for RF shielding and Electromagnetic Interference (EMI) control is an integral part of developing modern electronic systems. Whether it's a consumer device, industrial equipment, or military technology, ensuring that a product is resistant to unwanted interference and does not emit excessive EMI is critical for its performance, safety, and compliance with regulatory standards. This chapter explores the best practices for product design that incorporates RF shielding and EMI control, from selecting the right materials to integrating shielding strategies in circuit boards and enclosures. It also examines simulation tools that help predict and analyze EMI/EMC behavior during the design phase.

Best Practices for Product Design to Prevent EMI

Design for Minimal EMI Emissions:

- **Proper Grounding**: A well-designed grounding system is essential in reducing the impact of EMI. All electronic components should be connected to a single ground plane to ensure consistent reference voltages and avoid creating ground loops, which can increase EMI emissions.
- **Shielding Critical Components**: High-frequency components or those prone to emitting EMI, such as power supplies and microprocessors, should be shielded using appropriate materials like metal enclosures or conductive coatings. Using ferrite beads on power lines and signal lines can also help in reducing high-frequency EMI.
- **Twisted Pair Wiring**: Twisted pair cables, which consist of two wires twisted together, help cancel out electromagnetic interference, especially for signal transmission. This design reduces the loop area between wires, lowering susceptibility to EMI.
- **PCB Layout Considerations**: The layout of the printed circuit board (PCB) plays a critical role in managing EMI. Proper placement of components, routing of traces, and the use of decoupling capacitors close to sensitive components can minimize noise and improve performance. Avoiding long, unshielded trace runs can also reduce the loop areas that can radiate EMI.

Electromagnetic Compatibility (EMC) Design Principles:

- **Segregating High and Low Power Circuits**: Isolating high-power circuits (such as power supplies or motor controllers) from low-power circuits (such as microprocessors or analog sensors) can prevent high-frequency noise from coupling into sensitive components.
- **Use of Filters**: Filters (e.g., low-pass, high-pass, and band-pass) are essential in attenuating unwanted noise signals before they can enter or exit the system. Filters placed on power and signal lines are particularly effective in controlling EMI.
- **Minimizing EMI Radiated from Interconnects**: The physical design of connectors, cables, and interconnects can significantly influence EMI. Shielded cables, properly designed connectors, and minimizing cable lengths all help prevent radiation and reduce signal coupling between different system parts.
- **PCB Ground Planes**: A continuous ground plane provides a low-resistance path for current and helps shield sensitive components from external interference. Effective PCB grounding ensures that the system performs as intended and limits the risk of EMI emissions.

Integration of RF Shielding in Circuit Boards and Enclosures

RF shielding is often implemented both within the circuit board and at the system enclosure level. Below are key considerations for integrating RF shielding into both:

PCB Integration of Shielding:

- **Ground Plane Design**: A solid, uninterrupted ground plane is one of the most effective methods of shielding on a PCB. The ground plane provides a reference point for signals and helps absorb stray EMI.
- **Shielding Via Holes**: These holes can be used to connect ground planes on different layers of the PCB, ensuring that high-frequency EMI does not escape from one layer to another.
- **Shielding Gaskets and Covers**: In some cases, a conductive cover or a shielding gasket may be used on top of sensitive areas of the PCB to further reduce EMI. These materials provide a shield that reflects or absorbs electromagnetic energy.

System Enclosures and External Shielding:

- **Enclosures for RF Shielding**: Metal enclosures are commonly used to shield electronic systems from external electromagnetic interference. These enclosures block unwanted radiation from affecting sensitive circuits and can also prevent emissions from radiating into the environment. The material chosen for the enclosure, such as copper, aluminum, or stainless steel, should provide sufficient attenuation for the intended frequencies.
- **Faraday Cages**: A Faraday cage is a type of enclosure that surrounds the entire system in a conductive material to block electromagnetic fields. Faraday cages are often used in environments where strong protection from EMI is necessary, such as in medical or military equipment.
- **Gaskets and Conductive Seals**: Seals made of conductive materials like elastomers or metals can be placed at the junctions of enclosures to maintain the integrity of the shielding. These seals help prevent EMI from leaking through gaps or seams in the enclosure.
- **Ventilation Considerations**: For systems requiring airflow (e.g., for cooling purposes), it is important to design RF shielding that does not compromise ventilation. This can be done using specially designed conductive mesh or vents that allow airflow while still blocking electromagnetic radiation.

Design Considerations for High-Frequency Applications

In high-frequency applications (e.g., 5G, radar, and satellite communications), design considerations become even more critical. RF shielding and EMI control in these systems must be optimized for the unique challenges posed by high-frequency signals:

1. **Minimizing Signal Loss**: High-frequency signals are more susceptible to attenuation and signal loss. Designers must take care to minimize the path loss through proper impedance matching, shielding, and use of high-quality materials. Low-loss transmission lines and connectors, as well as controlled impedance traces on the PCB, are essential in high-frequency designs.
2. **Avoiding Crosstalk**: Crosstalk, or unwanted signal coupling between adjacent traces or circuits, is a significant concern in high-frequency applications. Shielding and careful routing of traces are necessary to reduce the possibility of crosstalk, particularly between high-speed signal traces and sensitive analog or power lines.
3. **Antenna Design and Placement**: For devices that include antennas, such as communication systems or IoT devices, careful design and placement of the antenna are crucial for minimizing interference. Antenna radiation patterns, orientation, and the materials surrounding the antenna should be considered in the shielding design.

Simulation Tools for EMI/EMC Analysis and Prediction

Simulation tools have become indispensable for EMI/EMC analysis during the design process. They allow engineers to predict how electromagnetic fields will behave in a product and to identify potential sources of interference before physical prototypes are built.

1. **Electromagnetic Simulation Software**: Programs like CST Studio Suite, COMSOL Multiphysics, and ANSYS HFSS allow designers to model and simulate the electromagnetic behavior of components, circuits, and enclosures. These tools help visualize how EMI will propagate through the system, identify potential sources of interference, and optimize shielding configurations.

2. **Time-Domain and Frequency-Domain Simulations**: Time-domain simulations are used to analyze transient events such as signal pulses, while frequency-domain simulations help assess how a system responds to continuous wave signals. Both are crucial for understanding how EMI affects different parts of the system.

3. **Full-EMC Simulation**: Some software tools provide full-system EMC analysis, including the integration of shielding, grounding, and circuit behavior, to ensure that a product meets all regulatory standards before it is manufactured.

4. **Coupling Analysis**: Coupling analysis helps identify where electromagnetic energy may leak from one part of the system to another, which is especially important for systems that are operating at high frequencies. Simulation tools can be used to analyze coupling through power lines, signal lines, and between different parts of the PCB.

Conclusion

Designing for RF shielding and EMI control is essential for ensuring that electronic systems operate effectively in today's increasingly connected and complex environments. By adhering to best practices in grounding, PCB layout, and enclosure design, engineers can reduce EMI emissions, increase system immunity to external interference, and ensure that products meet regulatory standards. High-frequency applications present unique challenges that require specialized approaches, and simulation tools are invaluable in predicting and resolving EMI/EMC issues during the design process. As electronic devices become more integrated and complex, incorporating robust EMI and RF shielding strategies will be crucial for the reliable performance of next-generation systems.

Chapter 12: Advanced Techniques in RF Jamming

RF jamming, as a critical aspect of modern electronic warfare and cybersecurity, has evolved significantly in recent years. As technologies advance, so do the methods used to disrupt and control radio frequency (RF) signals. This chapter will explore the most advanced techniques in RF jamming, including frequency hopping, spread spectrum jamming, smart jammers, and military-grade technologies. Additionally, we will explore how emerging technologies, such as artificial intelligence (AI), are shaping the future of RF jamming and its use in warfare and cybersecurity.

1. Frequency Hopping and Spread Spectrum Jamming

Frequency Hopping: Frequency hopping is a technique used to avoid detection and jamming by rapidly switching the transmission frequency. Instead of transmitting on a fixed frequency, a signal is rapidly switched across a broad spectrum according to a pre-determined or pseudo-random sequence. This makes it difficult for adversaries to jam the signal or intercept the communication, as the frequency is constantly changing.

- **Jamming Challenge:** Frequency hopping systems, like those used in military communications or certain wireless technologies, are resistant to traditional jamming because the jammer would need to follow the exact hopping pattern to disrupt communication.
- **Anti-Jamming Techniques:** To counteract frequency hopping, advanced jammers can attempt to locate the frequency-hopping sequence, which is difficult without prior knowledge of the hopping pattern. To bypass this, sophisticated jammers use algorithms that mimic or predict frequency patterns based on statistical analysis or intelligence about the system's operational parameters.

Spread Spectrum Jamming: Spread spectrum technology spreads the signal across a wide frequency band, making it difficult to detect and jam. It's often used in military applications and secure communications, such as GPS and Bluetooth, because of its resilience against interference and eavesdropping.

Types of Spread Spectrum:

- **Direct Sequence Spread Spectrum (DSSS):** The original signal is multiplied by a spreading code, which spreads the energy over a wide band.
- **Frequency Hopping Spread Spectrum (FHSS):** The signal hops between different frequencies at regular intervals, as mentioned above.

Jamming Techniques for Spread Spectrum:

2. Smart Jammers: Adaptive Systems and AI-Driven Interference

The next generation of jammers moves beyond basic interference techniques and leverages artificial intelligence (AI) to dynamically adapt to the environment and optimize disruption strategies. These "smart jammers" are capable of detecting, analyzing, and responding to signals in real time, making them much more effective in complex RF environments.

- **Real-Time Signal Analysis:** AI-powered jammers use machine learning algorithms to analyze incoming signals and identify the most vulnerable frequencies or communication patterns. By adapting to the environment, smart jammers can target only specific signals, ensuring minimal collateral interference with other communications.

- **Adaptive Jamming:** Adaptive jamming systems are capable of altering their characteristics (e.g., frequency, power, modulation) in response to the countermeasures deployed by the target system. This makes these jammers much harder to detect and counter. They can selectively block communication while allowing others to function, a significant advantage over traditional jamming techniques.

- **Cognitive Radio and Smart Jamming:** Cognitive radio systems are designed to dynamically adjust the frequency and modulation schemes to avoid interference. Smart jammers can target these systems by identifying cognitive radio "holes" and exploiting vulnerabilities in real-time. By understanding the communication strategies of a cognitive radio, smart jammers can disrupt specific frequencies or communication protocols with precision.

3. Military-Grade RF Jamming Technologies

Military-grade jamming technologies are designed to handle complex RF environments and engage multiple targets simultaneously. These systems are often deployed in electronic warfare operations, where they are used to incapacitate or neutralize enemy communications, radar, and navigation systems.

- **Directed Energy Weapons (DEWs):** Directed energy jamming systems use focused energy (like microwaves or lasers) to disable electronic devices. High-powered microwave (HPM) weapons can generate intense electromagnetic fields that disrupt or destroy sensitive RF systems. HPM systems can be targeted at specific components, such as communications satellites or radar systems, without causing widespread collateral damage.
- **Broadband Jammers:** Military broadband jammers are capable of emitting interference across a wide range of frequencies, making them useful for disrupting a broad spectrum of communications. These jammers work by overwhelming the entire frequency range, forcing communication systems to operate erratically or fail.
- **Counter-Radar Jamming:** Radar systems are a critical component of military operations, and jamming radar signals is a key tactic in electronic warfare. Military jammers use a variety of techniques to disable or confuse radar systems, including:

- **Noise Jamming:** Broadcasting random noise across the radar's frequency to mask the radar signal.
- **Deceptive Jamming:** Introducing false signals or "ghost" targets into the radar system to mislead the operator.
- **Expendable Decoys:** Using chaff or flares to scatter electromagnetic signals and create confusion, making it difficult for the radar system to lock onto a target.

Communication Jamming in Military Operations:

4. RF Jamming in Cybersecurity and Warfare

As cyber warfare becomes increasingly important, RF jamming technologies are being integrated into cybersecurity strategies. The ability to disrupt communication and navigation systems through RF interference has profound implications for national security and warfare tactics.

- **Cyber-Physical Attacks:** In cybersecurity, RF jamming can be used as part of a broader cyber-physical attack, targeting critical infrastructure. For example, jamming GPS signals can disrupt navigation systems, leading to significant consequences in military and civilian applications.
- **Satellite Jamming:** The global reliance on satellite communication and positioning systems, such as GPS, has led to the development of jamming technologies specifically designed to block or deceive satellite signals. These jammers use powerful signals to overwhelm satellite receivers, preventing them from receiving critical data.
- **Jamming in Urban Warfare:** In urban environments, where RF communication is heavily relied upon, jamming systems are deployed to disrupt enemy operations. Jammers can target wireless communication between troops, drones, and other electronic assets, preventing coordination and rendering enemies' communications ineffective.

5. The Future of RF Jamming in Warfare and Cybersecurity

The future of RF jamming in warfare and cybersecurity will see increased sophistication, with AI and machine learning playing a central role in evolving jamming technologies. As RF systems become more complex and widespread, adversaries will continue to develop smarter, more adaptable jammers that are harder to detect and counter.

- **Quantum Computing and Jamming:** Quantum computing has the potential to revolutionize RF jamming by enabling the processing of vast amounts of RF data in real time. Quantum algorithms could predict and disrupt signals with unprecedented accuracy, making it a potent tool for future RF jamming technologies.

- **5G Networks and Jamming:** The rollout of 5G networks will increase the complexity of RF communication systems. As these systems become more advanced, jammers will need to develop techniques to disrupt high-frequency signals in the millimeter-wave bands used by 5G, requiring new methods of interference and signal prediction.

- **AI-Driven Countermeasures:** With the increasing use of AI in RF jamming systems, defensive measures will also become more advanced. AI-driven countermeasures will be employed to detect jamming attempts in real-time and dynamically switch frequencies or protocols to avoid disruption.

- **Regulatory Challenges and Ethical Concerns:** The continued development of RF jamming technologies raises significant ethical and legal questions. The use of jammers to interfere with public communication systems or critical infrastructure could have unintended consequences. Future regulations will need to balance the tactical advantages of jamming with the potential risks to civilian safety and privacy.

Conclusion

Advanced techniques in RF jamming, from frequency hopping and spread spectrum jamming to smart jammers and military-grade technologies, have dramatically reshaped modern warfare and cybersecurity. As jamming systems become increasingly sophisticated, they offer new strategic capabilities while also presenting new challenges. The integration of artificial intelligence and other emerging technologies will continue to evolve jamming techniques, providing even greater control over RF communication systems. As these technologies develop, their role in both defense and offense will be critical in shaping the future of cybersecurity, warfare, and the protection of critical infrastructure.

Chapter 13: Regulatory Standards and Compliance

As the use of RF technologies grows across various industries—from telecommunications and defense to consumer electronics—ensuring compliance with regulatory standards is essential for the safe and effective operation of RF systems. This chapter will explore the key international standards for electromagnetic interference (EMI) and electromagnetic compatibility (EMC), the legal frameworks governing RF jamming devices, regulatory testing and certification processes, and strategies for ensuring compliance in RF systems and products.

1. International Standards for EMI and EMC

EMI and EMC standards are critical for maintaining the integrity and reliability of electronic devices in today's interconnected world. These standards govern the acceptable levels of interference that devices can generate or experience, ensuring that devices do not disrupt each other's operation or cause unsafe conditions in sensitive environments.

Key Regulatory Bodies:

- **Federal Communications Commission (FCC) [USA]:** The FCC is responsible for managing the use of the electromagnetic spectrum in the United States, establishing rules and standards for preventing harmful interference between devices. FCC regulations, such as the Title 47 of the Code of Federal Regulations (CFR) Part 15, define the limits for radiated emissions and conducted emissions from electronic devices.
- **International Electrotechnical Commission (IEC):** The IEC is a global organization that publishes international standards for electrical and electronic technologies, including EMI and EMC standards. The IEC 61000 series is the most commonly referenced set of standards for EMC, detailing testing methods and limits for emission and immunity levels.
- **European Union (CE Marking):** In Europe, CE marking is required for products that fall within the scope of EMC Directive (2014/30/EU), which sets limits on electromagnetic emissions and immunity for devices. CE marking ensures that the product complies with the EMC regulations, and manufacturers must meet specific technical standards.
- **Telecommunications Industry Association (TIA):** The TIA is a standards development organization focused on communication technologies. The TIA-968-A standard outlines requirements for telecommunications equipment, including emission and immunity levels.

- **Institute of Electrical and Electronics Engineers (IEEE):** The IEEE is an important contributor to the development of global standards in electronics and communications. IEEE standards, such as IEEE 802.11 (Wi-Fi) and IEEE 802.3 (Ethernet), include provisions for EMI and EMC.

EMC Testing Standards:

- **IEC 61000-4-3:** This standard defines immunity testing for radiated electromagnetic fields and outlines test procedures to determine how devices withstand RF interference.
- **IEC 61000-4-6:** Specifies testing methods for immunity to conducted disturbances on signal and power lines.
- **ISO 11452:** Focuses on testing automotive electronics for EMC, including RF susceptibility tests for vehicles.

2. Legal Frameworks Governing the Use of Jamming Devices

While RF jamming has legitimate applications, such as military operations and spectrum management, the use of jamming devices is highly regulated due to their potential to disrupt critical communications. Legal restrictions on jamming vary by country, and unauthorized jamming can lead to severe penalties.

United States:

- **Communications Act of 1934 (FCC Title II):** The use of jamming devices is prohibited under the Communications Act. The FCC specifically forbids the use of any device that interferes with the lawful use of communication services, including cell phone signals, GPS, and Wi-Fi. Violators can face fines up to $112,500 per violation and potential imprisonment.
- **FCC Rule on Jamming Devices (47 CFR § 15.1):** This rule prohibits any individual or entity from operating a jamming device that intentionally interferes with the operation of a radio frequency communication service. The use of jammers is generally restricted to authorized government agencies, such as military and law enforcement, under specific circumstances.

European Union:

- **Radio Equipment Directive (2014/53/EU):** The use of jammers is prohibited in the European Union under the Radio Equipment Directive. Devices that intentionally interfere with the operation of radio communications must not be marketed or used within the EU. Exceptions exist for government-authorized agencies under controlled conditions.
- **EMC Directive (2014/30/EU):** The EMC Directive prohibits the marketing and use of equipment that does not comply with EMC standards. This includes devices that generate harmful interference or are vulnerable to interference themselves.

International Considerations:

International Telecommunication Union (ITU):

Military and Government Exceptions:

In some cases, military or government agencies are exempt from certain regulations regarding jamming. These organizations may be authorized to use jamming technologies for national security, law enforcement, and defense purposes. However, the deployment of such systems is often heavily regulated and requires government approval.

3. Regulatory Testing and Certification Processes

To ensure that electronic devices comply with EMC and EMI standards, regulatory testing and certification processes are essential. These tests determine whether a product meets the required emissions and immunity thresholds, ensuring it will not cause harmful interference in its operating environment.

Testing Laboratories:

Accredited Testing Facilities:

Types of EMC Tests:

- **Emission Testing:** This includes measuring both radiated and conducted emissions to ensure that the product does not emit interference beyond the legal limits. Tests measure the level of RF emissions generated by the device under normal operating conditions.
- **Immunity Testing:** This evaluates how a device responds to external electromagnetic interference. It tests how well a device can function when exposed to RF fields, conducted disturbances, or electrostatic discharge (ESD).
- **Radiated Emission Testing:** Performed in an anechoic chamber, this test measures the RF emissions radiated from a product to ensure compliance with the relevant emission limits set by regulatory bodies.
- **Conducted Emission Testing:** Involves measuring the emissions that travel along power lines or other cables connected to the device. This is particularly important for devices connected to electrical grids or communication networks.

Certification Marks:

- **CE Marking (EU):** Products that meet EMC requirements in the European Union must bear the CE marking. The CE mark signifies that the product conforms to the necessary EMC and safety standards.
- **FCC Marking (USA):** In the United States, devices that meet the FCC's EMC requirements must be tested and certified by an authorized body. The device will then bear an FCC mark indicating compliance.
- **UL Certification:** While not always specific to EMC, Underwriters Laboratories (UL) certification ensures that a product meets safety and operational standards, including some relevant EMC criteria.

4. Ensuring Compliance in RF Systems and Products

Compliance with RF and EMI regulations is not only essential for legal and safety reasons but also for ensuring the reliability of devices in complex RF environments. Organizations must follow best practices in both design and testing to meet regulatory requirements.

Designing for Compliance:

- **Early Integration of EMC Considerations:** Designers should consider EMC factors from the early stages of product development. This includes selecting appropriate materials for shielding, grounding, and filtering to minimize emissions and improve immunity.
- **Component Selection:** Choosing components with low emission levels or higher immunity ratings can help in meeting EMC standards. Low-noise oscillators, shields, and high-quality power supplies can reduce unwanted emissions.
- **Simulation Tools:** Simulation tools for electromagnetic field analysis, such as finite element method (FEM) solvers and electromagnetic compatibility analysis software, can help predict EMI and EMC behavior in the design phase. These tools can also help optimize shielding effectiveness and minimize the potential for interference.

Testing and Certification:

- **Pre-Certification Testing:** Conducting in-house or third-party pre-certification testing can identify potential EMC issues before the formal certification process. This helps avoid delays or failed certifications.
- **Post-Compliance Monitoring:** After certification, regular monitoring and retesting are necessary to ensure that products continue to meet EMC standards, particularly after any design updates or component changes.

Documentation and Reporting:

- **Compliance Documentation:** Manufacturers must maintain detailed records of compliance testing, including test reports, simulation data, and certifications. These documents are essential for demonstrating compliance during regulatory inspections or audits.
- **Regulatory Changes:** Staying updated on evolving regulations and standards is crucial for maintaining compliance. Manufacturers should continuously monitor changes in regional and international regulations to adapt their products as necessary.

Conclusion

Regulatory standards and compliance play a critical role in the development and deployment of RF systems. From ensuring that electronic devices do not interfere with other systems to adhering to legal frameworks governing the use of jamming devices, understanding and adhering to international standards is essential. By incorporating early design considerations for EMI and EMC control, utilizing accredited testing facilities, and obtaining necessary certifications, manufacturers can ensure their products meet regulatory requirements and perform reliably in complex RF environments.

Chapter 14: RF Interference in Industrial and Commercial Systems

Radio Frequency (RF) interference poses a significant threat to the functionality and safety of industrial and commercial systems, where sensitive operations and critical infrastructures are often reliant on precise and uninterrupted communication. From manufacturing plants to hospitals, RF interference can compromise performance, efficiency, and even safety. In this chapter, we will explore the sources of RF interference in industrial environments, the impact it has on industrial control systems (ICS) and automation, its effects on medical devices, and the strategies used to address and mitigate EMI in critical infrastructure.

1. Sources of RF Interference in Industrial Environments

RF interference in industrial settings can originate from a variety of sources, both internal and external to the facility. These sources can disrupt control systems, automation processes, and communication links, leading to operational inefficiencies, malfunctions, or even dangerous situations.

Common Internal Sources of RF Interference:

- **Electrical Equipment:** High-power machinery, motors, transformers, and industrial computers can emit electromagnetic fields that interfere with sensitive communication systems. Equipment such as variable frequency drives (VFDs) or large electrical loads often generates harmonics and other forms of RF noise.

- **Welding Equipment:** Welding machines and arc welders, due to the high energy and electrical discharge they generate, can radiate significant electromagnetic interference.

- **Heavy Machinery and Motors:** Large industrial motors, pumps, and compressors that run on alternating current can create significant electromagnetic fields. These devices often induce voltage spikes, resulting in RF emissions.

- **Power Supplies and Inverters:** Switching power supplies and inverters, used in many industrial applications for converting power, can produce high-frequency emissions that interfere with surrounding electronic systems.

Common External Sources of RF Interference:

- **Nearby Radio Transmissions:** Industrial plants located near broadcasting stations, airports, or other RF transmission towers may experience interference from high-powered radio signals.
- **Cellular Networks:** Mobile phones and base stations can create localized interference, especially in environments with many wireless communication devices.
- **Satellite Communication Signals:** In certain industrial environments, especially those that involve high-precision equipment like radar or telemetry, satellite communication signals may interfere with RF-sensitive systems.

2. Impact of RF Interference on Industrial Control Systems (ICS) and Automation

Industrial control systems (ICS) are the backbone of manufacturing processes, utilities, and infrastructure. They involve the use of automated systems for controlling machinery, monitoring processes, and ensuring that operations run smoothly. RF interference can disrupt these systems in several ways:

Degraded Signal Integrity: RF interference can corrupt the data transmitted between control systems, sensors, and actuators. In systems that rely on wireless protocols (e.g., Wi-Fi, Zigbee, Bluetooth, or proprietary RF systems), the introduction of noise can result in data packet loss, delays, or errors. In highly sensitive industrial applications, even minor data corruption can lead to failures in system operations or unsafe conditions.

Miscommunication and False Signals: RF interference can cause control systems to receive incorrect or false signals. This is particularly dangerous in automation processes that rely on real-time data for decision-making. For example, in automated manufacturing lines, false sensor readings or erroneous actuator commands could result in misalignment, product defects, or damage to machinery.

Disruptions to Remote Monitoring and SCADA Systems: Supervisory Control and Data Acquisition (SCADA) systems are widely used to monitor and control industrial processes, often across large geographic areas. RF interference can lead to communication dropouts or delayed responses between the central control room and remote devices. Such disruptions can delay critical decision-making and hinder the ability to respond to emergencies or faults in a timely manner.

Impact on Process Control Systems: Many industrial plants rely on real-time process control systems for temperature, pressure, and flow regulation. RF interference can distort the signals received by controllers, leading to incorrect control outputs and potential deviations from optimal operating conditions. This can result in inefficient energy use, product quality issues, or even hazardous situations.

3. RF Interference in Medical Devices

RF interference is particularly concerning in medical environments, where device malfunction can directly impact patient safety. Many medical devices, such as pacemakers, infusion pumps, MRI machines, and X-ray equipment, rely on RF signals for communication or operation.

Pacemakers and Implantable Devices: RF interference can disrupt the operation of pacemakers or other implantable medical devices, leading to malfunctions that could endanger patients. For example, strong RF signals from nearby MRI machines, mobile phones, or radio transmitters can potentially alter the programming of these devices, causing erratic behavior or even shutting them down.

Hospital Equipment and Wireless Communication: Hospitals increasingly use wireless communication technologies to track patient data, manage medical devices, and communicate between staff. RF interference can disrupt wireless communication networks, causing delays in the transmission of critical information. For instance, interference can slow down the transfer of medical images from diagnostic equipment or result in missed alarms from monitoring systems, both of which could compromise patient care.

Impact on Diagnostic Equipment: Devices such as electrocardiograms (ECGs), ultrasound machines, and MRI scanners are highly sensitive to external electromagnetic fields. RF interference can degrade the quality of diagnostic signals, leading to inaccurate results. In some cases, this can delay diagnoses or lead to incorrect medical treatments.

4. Addressing EMI in Critical Infrastructure

Critical infrastructure—such as power grids, water treatment plants, transportation networks, and communication systems—relies on robust, interference-free operation to ensure public safety and national security. RF interference can pose significant risks to these systems, making it crucial to implement effective EMI mitigation strategies.

Power Grid Protection: The electrical power grid is especially vulnerable to RF interference. High-voltage lines and substations can act as antennas, radiating electromagnetic waves that can affect nearby communication systems or be susceptible to external RF signals. To mitigate these risks, power grids are increasingly using advanced shielding, grounding techniques, and filtering solutions to prevent harmful interference from affecting system performance.

Water Treatment Facilities: In water treatment plants, automation systems and remote sensors are often used to monitor water quality and manage chemical dosing. RF interference could cause erroneous readings, affecting the ability to treat water effectively. To mitigate this, RF shielding and filtering are incorporated into system designs to protect sensitive equipment and ensure continuous monitoring.

Transportation and Traffic Control Systems: Transportation networks depend on reliable communication between control centers, vehicles, and infrastructure (e.g., traffic signals, toll booths). RF interference can disrupt the communication protocols used in modern traffic management systems, leading to delays or safety hazards. To safeguard against this, transportation systems implement EMI shielding for both wired and wireless components.

Use of Encryption and Secure Communication: As part of the broader strategy to protect critical infrastructure from RF interference, encryption and secure communication protocols are often employed. These measures ensure that even if RF interference affects the communication channel, the integrity and security of the transmitted data are maintained. For example, military and government systems often use frequency-hopping spread spectrum (FHSS) techniques to make it difficult for RF jamming signals to interfere with critical communications.

5. Strategies for Mitigating RF Interference in Industrial and Commercial Systems

The implementation of robust RF shielding, signal suppression, and EMI protection techniques is vital for safeguarding industrial and commercial systems from the detrimental effects of RF interference. Here are key strategies:

RF Shielding: Shielding is one of the most effective ways to prevent RF interference from entering or leaving sensitive equipment. Faraday cages, conductive enclosures, and shielding tapes or coatings are commonly used in industrial and commercial systems. These materials are designed to block or attenuate the passage of electromagnetic waves, preventing external interference from impacting the system or internal emissions from radiating outside the facility.

Filtering: Filters can be installed at various points in the system to reduce EMI. Low-pass filters, band-pass filters, and ferrite beads can be used to suppress unwanted RF signals and prevent them from propagating through circuits or power lines.

Grounding and Bonding: Proper grounding and bonding are essential in reducing EMI in industrial environments. A well-designed grounding system ensures that any stray electromagnetic energy is safely dissipated, preventing it from interfering with sensitive components. Bonding metal structures together can also help eliminate potential differences that may cause RF interference.

RF-Absorbing Materials: Using materials that absorb RF energy—such as ferrite cores, conductive gaskets, or absorptive coatings—can help minimize interference by reducing the reflection of electromagnetic waves within the system.

Redundancy and Resilience: In critical systems, redundancy is a key approach to mitigating the impact of RF interference. By incorporating backup communication channels, error correction techniques, and failover mechanisms, systems can continue to operate effectively even when one channel is disrupted by EMI.

Regular Testing and Monitoring: Continuous monitoring and regular testing of RF interference levels help identify potential threats and ensure that EMI protection strategies are effective. Spectrum analyzers and EMI test equipment can be used to detect sources of interference and verify compliance with industry standards.

Conclusion

RF interference in industrial and commercial systems presents a significant challenge to the smooth operation of critical infrastructure, medical equipment, and automation systems. By understanding the sources and impacts of RF interference, industries can implement effective strategies to mitigate its effects. Shielding, filtering, proper grounding, and the use of secure communication protocols are crucial tools in safeguarding operations from unwanted electromagnetic disruptions. As industries become increasingly reliant on interconnected systems and automation, the importance of managing RF interference will only continue to grow, requiring ongoing innovation and vigilance to ensure the reliability and safety of modern technological ecosystems.

Chapter 15: Signal Integrity in High-Speed Communication Systems

In today's rapidly evolving technological landscape, high-speed communication systems have become a cornerstone of modern infrastructure. From 5G networks and satellite communication to high-frequency trading platforms and real-time data streaming, the need for reliable and clear signal transmission is critical. However, maintaining signal integrity in such systems is a formidable challenge, especially when the environment is subject to electromagnetic interference (EMI) and RF jamming. This chapter will explore the principles of signal integrity, the challenges faced in high-frequency signal transmission, tools and techniques to ensure signal integrity, and how RF jamming and EMI affect signal quality.

1. Principles of Signal Integrity in RF Systems

Signal integrity refers to the quality of an electrical signal as it travels through a system. It is concerned with maintaining the signal's original characteristics, ensuring that the transmitted information is accurate, and minimizing any distortion, degradation, or interference that can corrupt the signal.

In RF systems, signal integrity is affected by factors such as:

- **Attenuation:** Loss of signal strength as it propagates through a medium or across components. This is a primary concern in long-distance or high-frequency signal transmission.
- **Reflection:** Occurs when part of the signal is reflected back toward the source due to impedance mismatches in transmission lines or connectors. Reflections cause interference, leading to signal degradation.
- **Crosstalk:** Unwanted coupling of signals between adjacent conductors or circuits. This is common in densely packed circuit boards or cables, leading to signal degradation.
- **Distortion:** Any modification of the signal's waveform, which can lead to errors in data transmission. Nonlinearities in components or devices, such as amplifiers, can introduce distortion.
- **Noise:** External electromagnetic noise from various sources, including power supplies, motors, or nearby RF sources, can superimpose on the desired signal, causing interference.

To preserve signal integrity, the system must be designed to minimize these factors and ensure the signal remains stable and undistorted as it travels through its communication path.

2. High-Frequency Signal Transmission and Its Challenges

As communication systems scale to higher frequencies—whether it's for 5G networks, Wi-Fi 6, or advanced radar systems—the challenges of signal integrity become even more pronounced. High-frequency signals have shorter wavelengths, which make them more susceptible to the following issues:

- **Skin Effect:** At higher frequencies, signals tend to travel on the surface of conductors rather than throughout the entire cross-section. This phenomenon, known as the skin effect, increases resistance, leading to greater signal loss and heat dissipation.
- **Signal Propagation Losses:** As the frequency increases, the signal is more likely to suffer from propagation losses due to factors such as the conductivity and permittivity of the materials the signal passes through. This can be exacerbated in outdoor environments with weather-related factors like rain, snow, or atmospheric moisture.
- **Increased Susceptibility to EMI:** Higher frequencies are more likely to encounter interference from both intentional and unintentional RF sources. At high frequencies, even minor EMI can significantly affect signal quality, especially when dealing with very weak signals or long-distance transmissions.
- **Interference from Multipath Propagation:** In environments with reflective surfaces, signals may take multiple paths to reach the receiver. This can lead to constructive or destructive interference, where signals add up (constructively) or cancel each other out (destructively), resulting in signal degradation.

Addressing these challenges requires precision design and advanced signal processing techniques to ensure clear and accurate transmission of high-frequency signals.

3. Tools and Techniques to Ensure Signal Integrity

Several tools and techniques are employed to ensure the integrity of signals in high-speed RF systems. These methods focus on minimizing losses, reflections, crosstalk, and external interference while maintaining signal clarity.

Signal Integrity Tools:

- **Time Domain Reflectometer (TDR):** This device is used to detect impedance mismatches, reflections, and other transmission line issues. By analyzing the time it takes for a reflected signal to return, engineers can pinpoint and correct signal integrity problems.
- **Network Analyzers:** Vector network analyzers (VNAs) measure the frequency response and characteristics of components and transmission lines. They help assess signal loss, phase shift, and impedance matching, ensuring that signals maintain their integrity across different frequencies.
- **Oscilloscopes:** High-speed oscilloscopes allow engineers to visualize signal waveforms, analyze signal quality, and detect timing errors, jitter, and other anomalies in real time. Modern oscilloscopes can capture signals at very high sample rates, allowing detailed analysis of high-frequency communications.

Design Considerations:

- **Impedance Matching:** To minimize reflections, it's essential to match the impedance of the transmission line (whether coaxial cable, microstrip, or other media) with that of the source and load. Proper impedance matching ensures maximum power transfer and minimizes signal loss.
- **PCB Layout Optimization:** For high-speed circuits, the layout of the PCB must be optimized to minimize noise, reflections, and crosstalk. Proper trace routing, controlled impedance, and ground plane design are essential to preserving signal integrity.
- **Shielding and Grounding:** Shielding can prevent EMI from entering sensitive components, while grounding minimizes noise and helps eliminate voltage spikes. A well-grounded design reduces the potential for signal interference.
- **Differential Signaling:** Using differential signals (where two complementary signals are transmitted on separate lines) is another way to preserve signal integrity, especially at high frequencies. Differential signaling is more robust against external noise and common-mode interference.

Active Components:

- **Buffers and Drivers:** Active components like buffers and drivers can help strengthen weak signals, ensuring they maintain integrity as they propagate through the system. These components ensure that the signal doesn't degrade over long distances or through lossy mediums.
- **Equalization and Compensation:** In systems where signal loss occurs, equalization techniques can restore the signal's amplitude and phase characteristics to their original state. For example, adaptive equalizers in communication receivers can correct for distortion caused by multipath propagation or channel imperfections.

4. How RF Jamming and EMI Affect Signal Quality

RF jamming and electromagnetic interference (EMI) are significant threats to the quality of high-speed signals, especially in critical systems such as communication networks, radar, and avionics. These external disturbances can cause severe degradation in signal quality, leading to:

- **Loss of Data Integrity:** Jamming introduces noise that can corrupt or completely destroy the transmitted data, rendering communication channels unreliable. This is particularly problematic in systems where accurate and error-free data transmission is paramount, such as financial networks, control systems, and military operations.
- **Latency and Signal Delays:** EMI can cause delays in signal transmission or introduce jitter (timing irregularities), resulting in reduced performance. This is especially critical in real-time systems, such as voice communication, video streaming, and radar systems, where timing is crucial.
- **Reduced Range and Coverage:** RF interference can reduce the effective range of a communication system. In wireless communication, EMI can cause signal attenuation, leading to lower signal strength and less reliable communication, especially in densely populated environments.
- **Loss of Signal Lock:** In satellite and GPS systems, RF interference can prevent receivers from locking onto signals, causing outages or navigation errors. Even weak interference can prevent satellite signals from being processed correctly, resulting in a failure of position accuracy.

To mitigate the effects of RF jamming and EMI on signal integrity, several countermeasures are employed:

- **Adaptive Filters and Noise Cancellation:** These techniques are used to minimize the effects of jamming and interference by selectively filtering out unwanted signals while preserving the integrity of the desired signal.
- **Spread Spectrum Techniques:** Methods like frequency hopping and direct sequence spread spectrum (DSSS) allow communication systems to spread their signals across a wide frequency band, making them less susceptible to narrowband jamming and interference.
- **Error Correction Codes (ECC):** In many high-speed communication systems, ECC is used to detect and correct errors in transmitted data, ensuring that the received signal remains intact even in the presence of interference.
- **Redundant Channels:** Some critical systems use multiple communication channels to ensure continuous operation. If one channel is jammed or interfered with, data can be rerouted through another, ensuring system reliability.

Conclusion

Maintaining signal integrity in high-speed communication systems is a complex and essential task, particularly in an age where RF jamming and EMI are growing concerns. High-frequency signal transmission presents unique challenges, including attenuation, reflections, and interference, but with careful design and the use of specialized tools, these challenges can be mitigated. Techniques such as impedance matching, shielding, differential signaling, and adaptive filtering are crucial to ensuring the reliable transmission of signals. As RF jamming and EMI continue to evolve, so too will the methods employed to protect and enhance the integrity of critical communication systems, ensuring they remain robust and resilient in increasingly complex electromagnetic environments.

Chapter 16: Future Trends in RF Shielding and EMI Control

The rapid advancements in technology are shaping the future of RF shielding and electromagnetic interference (EMI) control. As the demand for faster, more reliable communication systems grows, the challenges associated with RF interference and signal degradation are becoming more complex. This chapter explores the emerging technologies, the role of artificial intelligence (AI), the impact of quantum computing, and the evolution of smart shielding solutions in RF and EMI control. Understanding these trends is critical for professionals working to safeguard sensitive communication systems against interference in the coming years.

1. Emerging Technologies in Shielding Materials and Methods

Shielding technologies have made significant strides in recent years, evolving to meet the demands of increasingly sophisticated communication systems. New materials and innovative methods are being developed to provide more effective and efficient solutions for protecting sensitive electronics from RF interference.

Graphene and Carbon-Based Materials: Graphene, a single layer of carbon atoms arranged in a two-dimensional honeycomb lattice, is one of the most promising materials for next-generation RF shielding. Its exceptional electrical conductivity, high strength, and flexibility make it ideal for use in shielding applications. Researchers are exploring ways to integrate graphene into flexible substrates, offering the potential for lightweight, stretchable RF shielding materials that could be applied to a variety of devices, including wearables and portable electronics.

Carbon nanotubes (CNTs) and other carbon-based materials are also being explored for their high surface area, conductivity, and mechanical properties. CNT-based shielding materials offer excellent thermal and electrical conductivity, enabling them to effectively attenuate high-frequency interference while remaining lightweight and compact.

Metamaterials: Metamaterials are engineered materials with properties that do not exist in naturally occurring substances. By manipulating the structure of these materials on a microscopic scale, it is possible to create shielding that can block specific frequencies of RF radiation with a level of precision that conventional materials cannot achieve.

Metamaterials have the potential to improve the performance of RF shielding in areas such as wireless communication, radar, and satellite systems. These materials can be designed to operate over specific frequency ranges or to be highly selective, targeting interference sources while allowing desired signals to pass through with minimal attenuation.

Hybrid Shielding Materials: The combination of metallic and non-metallic materials is becoming increasingly popular in RF shielding. Hybrid materials leverage the advantages of both categories, creating shielding systems that are both highly effective and cost-efficient. For example, using carbon-based materials in combination with traditional metals like copper or aluminum can result in lighter, more flexible shields with similar or superior attenuation performance. Hybrid shielding materials are especially useful for applications where flexibility, weight, and form factor are critical, such as in aerospace and wearable electronics.

2. The Role of Artificial Intelligence (AI) in Managing EMI and RF Interference

Artificial Intelligence (AI) is increasingly being integrated into RF shielding and EMI management systems. AI can optimize the detection, analysis, and mitigation of RF interference in real-time, offering more dynamic and adaptable solutions for shielding and signal integrity management.

Adaptive Shielding Systems: AI-driven adaptive shielding systems have the ability to dynamically adjust shielding parameters based on real-time monitoring of the electromagnetic environment. For example, AI algorithms can analyze the strength and frequency of incoming RF interference and adjust the shielding material or configuration to block only the harmful interference, while allowing the desired signal to pass through.

This dynamic approach is particularly useful in environments with fluctuating RF conditions, such as busy urban areas with heavy wireless traffic or military environments with active electronic warfare. By using machine learning and pattern recognition, AI systems can predict interference patterns and proactively adjust shielding and signal processing systems to mitigate future interference.

AI-Based EMI Detection and Analysis: AI can also improve the detection and classification of EMI sources. Traditional EMI detection systems often require human intervention to interpret data and identify the source of interference. AI systems can automate this process, analyzing large volumes of spectral data in real-time and pinpointing the source of interference with high accuracy. These systems can be used to monitor industrial environments, communication networks, or defense systems, allowing for faster response times and more efficient mitigation strategies.

Furthermore, AI-based models can identify patterns in EMI that may not be immediately apparent to human operators, leading to more accurate predictions and preemptive actions. Machine learning algorithms can continually improve their detection capabilities by learning from past interference events, optimizing shielding techniques and filtering methods over time.

3. Quantum Computing and Its Potential Impacts on EMI

Quantum computing, while still in its infancy, is expected to have profound implications for RF and EMI control. Quantum computers operate on principles of quantum mechanics, allowing them to solve certain complex problems much faster than classical computers. This opens the door to new opportunities in the realm of EMI and RF interference management.

Quantum Sensing: Quantum sensors, leveraging quantum properties such as superposition and entanglement, offer unprecedented sensitivity and accuracy in detecting electromagnetic fields. These sensors could be used to detect even the smallest amounts of RF interference in a system, allowing for more precise EMI management and shielding design.

For example, quantum sensors could help identify sources of interference that are not detectable by traditional methods, enabling earlier detection and more effective mitigation strategies. The precision of quantum sensors could also improve the calibration of RF shielding systems, ensuring optimal performance and minimal signal degradation.

Quantum Communication and Secure Signal Transmission: Quantum computing may also play a role in the development of quantum communication networks, which promise to offer ultra-secure transmission channels that are immune to certain types of eavesdropping and interference. Quantum key distribution (QKD) protocols, which use quantum principles to secure communication, could be integrated with existing RF shielding technologies to create ultra-secure communication systems that are resistant to RF jamming and hacking attempts.

Though quantum communication is still in the research and development stage, its potential to revolutionize secure communications could redefine how we approach RF shielding and EMI control in the future. If successful, quantum-based communication systems could dramatically reduce the impact of RF interference on sensitive communications.

4. Smart Shielding Solutions and Adaptive Designs

The future of RF shielding is increasingly focused on adaptability, intelligence, and integration with other technologies. Smart shielding solutions combine advanced materials, AI, and real-time monitoring systems to create shielding solutions that can respond to changing environments and interference sources.

Active and Tunable Shielding: Active shielding technologies, which use powered components to create electromagnetic fields that cancel out incoming interference, are becoming more advanced. These systems are able to detect RF interference in real-time and generate an opposing signal that effectively neutralizes it. These adaptive systems can be used in high-performance communication systems, medical equipment, and military applications where interference is unpredictable and dynamic.

Wearable and Flexible Shielding: As wearable electronics become more pervasive, the need for lightweight, flexible shielding solutions is increasing. Researchers are developing flexible, stretchable, and even transparent shielding materials that can be integrated into clothing, accessories, and even the skin. These wearable shields would be capable of protecting individuals from harmful RF radiation while maintaining comfort and usability.

Integrated EMI Control in IoT Devices: The growing number of Internet of Things (IoT) devices presents unique challenges for EMI control, as these devices often operate in close proximity to each other and are vulnerable to interference. Future shielding solutions will likely integrate EMI control directly into the design of IoT devices, ensuring that they remain immune to interference while also being energy-efficient and cost-effective. By using smart, adaptive shielding systems that can adjust to environmental conditions, IoT devices will become more resilient and reliable in RF-dense environments.

5. Conclusion

The future of RF shielding and EMI control lies in the development of smarter, more adaptable, and highly efficient solutions that can meet the challenges of increasingly complex and high-speed communication systems. Emerging materials, AI-driven systems, and the potential of quantum technologies will play key roles in shaping the landscape of RF protection. As RF interference becomes more prevalent and sophisticated, the ability to dynamically adjust shielding and mitigate EMI in real-time will become essential for safeguarding sensitive systems. By staying ahead of these technological trends, engineers and professionals in the field will ensure the continued reliability and integrity of modern communication systems, from military applications to everyday wireless devices.

Chapter 17: Case Studies in EMI and RF Shielding

In this chapter, we examine several real-world case studies where electromagnetic interference (EMI) and RF shielding played a critical role in addressing interference issues across various industries. These case studies demonstrate how EMI can disrupt sensitive systems and how effective RF shielding and signal suppression strategies can mitigate such disruptions. By analyzing specific incidents and their resolutions, we can gain valuable insights into best practices for EMI control and shielding solutions.

1. Aerospace Industry: EMI in Aircraft Communication Systems

Problem: In the aerospace industry, electromagnetic interference (EMI) is a significant concern due to the complex integration of various communication systems and electronic devices within an aircraft. One of the most notable incidents involved a major airline experiencing intermittent communication failures between the cockpit and air traffic control. The issue was traced to interference from a new satellite communications system that was installed on the aircraft. The system inadvertently caused interference with critical communication frequencies used by the aircraft's radio systems.

Resolution: To resolve this issue, the aerospace manufacturer implemented a multi-step approach to identify and mitigate the interference:

- **Shielding Enhancement:** The installation of advanced shielding materials within the satellite communication system's enclosure, designed to contain and block RF emissions from the new system.
- **Electromagnetic Compatibility (EMC) Testing:** The aircraft underwent rigorous EMC testing to simulate various interference scenarios and identify potential weak points in the shielding.
- **Reconfiguration of Antenna Placement:** The placement of antennas was adjusted to ensure that the satellite communication system and radio systems operated on separate frequencies, reducing the risk of signal overlap and interference.

Outcome: The successful implementation of these RF shielding solutions and the reconfiguration of the communication systems ensured that the aircraft's communication systems operated without interference, improving both safety and reliability.

2. Automotive Industry: EMI in Autonomous Vehicles

Problem: As the automotive industry moves toward the widespread deployment of autonomous vehicles, EMI poses an increasing risk to the reliability of vehicle control systems. In one case, an autonomous vehicle's radar and LiDAR systems began malfunctioning due to interference from nearby RF communication signals. The vehicle's systems were unable to accurately detect obstacles in real time, putting the safety of passengers at risk.

Resolution: The automotive manufacturer took a comprehensive approach to mitigate EMI and protect critical vehicle systems:

- **Shielded Enclosures:** Sensitive components, such as radar and LiDAR sensors, were enclosed in high-quality shielding materials to prevent interference from external sources.
- **Signal Filtering:** Filters were installed in the signal paths of critical sensors to reject unwanted RF signals while allowing the necessary communication between the vehicle's sensors and control systems.
- **System Redundancy:** The manufacturer implemented redundant sensing systems (e.g., using both radar and LiDAR) to ensure the vehicle could still operate safely in the presence of EMI.

Outcome: These measures significantly reduced the impact of EMI on the vehicle's autonomous systems. The vehicle's sensors were able to function accurately in complex environments, improving safety and performance. This case highlights the importance of robust EMI mitigation techniques in the development of autonomous and connected vehicles.

3. Healthcare Industry: RF Interference in Medical Devices

Problem: In the healthcare sector, RF interference can be particularly hazardous, especially when it impacts critical medical devices like pacemakers, defibrillators, and MRI machines. A case was reported where a patient with a pacemaker experienced erratic heart rate readings during a routine visit to a hospital. Upon investigation, the source of the interference was traced to a nearby Wi-Fi router, which was emitting strong RF signals that affected the pacemaker's operation.

Resolution: To resolve this issue, the healthcare provider implemented a series of RF shielding and signal suppression strategies:

- **Faraday Cages:** The hospital installed Faraday cages in areas where sensitive medical devices, such as MRI machines and pacemaker monitoring systems, were used. These cages prevented external RF signals from penetrating the area, ensuring that sensitive equipment was shielded from interference.
- **Shielding for Medical Implants:** Patients with pacemakers and other implants were provided with additional shielding around their medical devices to protect them from potential interference. Hospitals also started providing guidelines for patients on the risks of RF exposure and where to avoid high-emission areas.
- **Frequency Management:** The hospital worked with device manufacturers to ensure that the operating frequencies of pacemakers and other critical medical devices were far away from common Wi-Fi channels, minimizing the risk of interference.

Outcome: By employing these shielding and suppression techniques, the hospital significantly reduced the risk of RF interference affecting medical devices. Pacemaker performance improved, and the hospital also raised awareness of the potential risks associated with RF interference in healthcare settings.

4. Industrial Control Systems: EMI in Manufacturing Plants

Problem: In an industrial manufacturing plant, an RF interference issue caused major disruptions in the operation of automated machinery. The plant used wireless communication systems to control machinery on the factory floor, but an unshielded industrial motor caused EMI that led to communication breakdowns and machinery malfunctions. The interference led to significant production delays and raised safety concerns.

Resolution: The plant's engineers implemented a combination of shielding and grounding techniques to resolve the issue:

- **Shielded Cables and Connectors:** The communication lines between the wireless control system and the machinery were re-routed and fitted with shielded cables to prevent EMI from leaking into the control signals.
- **Grounding and Bonding:** Grounding systems were upgraded to ensure that all metallic components, including motors and machinery, were properly grounded. This reduced the potential for radiated EMI.
- **EMI Filters:** EMI filters were installed on all power supply lines feeding the machinery. These filters prevented high-frequency noise from entering the system and ensured clean power was delivered to the equipment.

Outcome: The application of shielding, grounding, and filtering solutions successfully mitigated the EMI issues, and the plant was able to resume normal operations without interference. The case highlighted the importance of considering EMI in the design and operation of industrial control systems, particularly in environments with heavy machinery.

5. Telecommunications: EMI in 5G Networks

Problem: With the rollout of 5G networks, telecommunications companies face new challenges related to EMI. One of the most notable incidents occurred in a densely populated urban area, where high-density 5G base stations began to experience signal degradation due to interference from nearby electronic equipment. The interference was affecting not only 5G performance but also critical communications systems, including emergency services.

Resolution: The telecommunications company employed a multi-pronged approach to address the interference:

- **Selective Shielding of Base Stations:** The company upgraded the shielding around base station equipment to prevent external EMI from affecting performance. This included using advanced materials that provided higher attenuation at the frequencies used by 5G networks.
- **EMI Testing and Site Optimization:** Site engineers conducted extensive EMI testing to identify sources of interference in the vicinity of each base station. Based on the results, the company optimized the placement of base stations to avoid high-interference zones and reduce signal degradation.
- **Collaboration with Equipment Manufacturers:** Telecom companies worked closely with equipment manufacturers to ensure that new 5G devices were designed with built-in EMI protection features, including enhanced shielding and filtering systems.

Outcome: With these measures in place, the telecom company successfully reduced the EMI affecting the 5G network. The performance of both 5G and legacy systems improved, and emergency communication services were no longer disrupted. This case emphasized the importance of proactive EMI management in the deployment of next-generation networks.

6. Key Lessons Learned from Case Studies

- **Proactive EMI Testing:** Early and ongoing EMI testing is essential to identify potential issues before they escalate. Implementing rigorous EMC testing during design and before deployment can save significant time and cost.
- **Tailored Solutions:** Each industry has unique EMI challenges. Solutions should be tailored to address the specific needs of each sector. For example, shielding solutions that work in aerospace might not be as effective in a hospital or industrial setting.
- **Collaboration Across Sectors:** Successful EMI management often involves collaboration between manufacturers, engineers, regulatory bodies, and end-users. Shared knowledge and insights can help develop more effective shielding solutions and mitigation strategies.
- **Adaptability of Shielding Technologies:** Shielding materials and methods should evolve to address emerging challenges, such as those posed by 5G, IoT devices, and autonomous systems.

Conclusion

The case studies presented in this chapter demonstrate the critical importance of RF shielding and EMI control in ensuring the reliability and safety of communication and electronic systems across a range of industries. Whether in aerospace, automotive, healthcare, or telecommunications, effective EMI mitigation techniques are essential to prevent disruptions and protect sensitive equipment. By learning from these real-world examples, engineers and professionals can improve their understanding of EMI challenges and apply best practices to develop more robust and resilient systems.

Chapter 18: Practical Guide to RF Jamming Devices

Radio Frequency (RF) jamming is the deliberate disruption of communication systems by emitting powerful RF signals on the same frequency used by legitimate systems. It is widely used in military and defense applications but can also be employed in various other sectors for security, testing, and counter-surveillance. In this chapter, we provide a detailed, practical guide to RF jamming devices, focusing on their specifications, design considerations, operational scenarios, and legal and ethical considerations.

1. Overview of RF Jamming Devices

RF jamming devices are designed to disrupt or block the transmission of RF signals, making communication systems malfunction or completely inoperative. These devices can target a wide range of communication technologies, including cellular networks, Wi-Fi, GPS, radar, and satellite communication systems.

The key components of a typical RF jamming device include:

- **Oscillators:** These generate the jamming signals at the desired frequencies.
- **Amplifiers:** They boost the jamming signal's power to ensure sufficient range and effectiveness.
- **Antenna Systems:** Different types of antennas are used depending on the target frequency range and the desired coverage area (omnidirectional or directional antennas).
- **Power Supply:** Jammers require a stable power source, which can be battery-powered for portability or AC-powered for stationary use.

RF jammers can be broadly classified into the following categories:

- **Narrowband Jammers:** These jammers focus on a specific frequency or a narrow band of frequencies.
- **Wideband Jammers:** These devices cover a wide range of frequencies simultaneously, disrupting multiple communication systems at once.
- **Burst Jammers:** They transmit powerful RF pulses or bursts of energy over short periods to overload the target system.
- **Deceptive Jammers:** These jammers use signal manipulation techniques to deceive a receiver into accepting false or corrupted information.

The operational design of a jammer depends on the application, whether it's military, industrial, or consumer-based.

2. Design Considerations for Building Jamming Devices

When designing an RF jamming device, several factors must be considered to ensure its effectiveness, reliability, and compliance with relevant regulations. Below are the key design considerations:

a. Frequency Range

The first consideration is the frequency range of the target system. The jammer must be designed to operate on frequencies that overlap with the frequencies of the communication system to be jammed. For example, a GPS jammer must operate on the L1 frequency band used by civilian GPS signals (1575 MHz).

b. Power Output

The power output of the jammer determines its range and effectiveness. High-power jammers are capable of disrupting communication over a larger area, while low-power jammers are more focused. Power output must be carefully calculated to ensure that the jamming signal is strong enough to interfere with the target system without wasting energy or causing unnecessary collateral interference.

c. Antenna Design

Antennas are crucial to the performance of an RF jammer. The choice of antenna depends on factors like:

- **Directivity:** Directional antennas focus the jamming energy in a specific direction, while omnidirectional antennas spread it equally in all directions.
- **Gain:** Higher-gain antennas can direct more energy into the target area, increasing jamming efficiency.
- **Size and Portability:** Smaller antennas may be required for portable, handheld jammers, while larger antennas are used in fixed, high-power jamming systems.

d. Modulation Techniques

Jamming devices can use different modulation techniques to interfere with the target signal. Some common modulation schemes include:

- **Continuous Wave (CW) Jamming:** A steady signal that occupies a single frequency continuously.
- **Noise Jamming:** A broad-spectrum signal that floods the target frequency range with noise.
- **Pulse Jamming:** Pulsed signals that disrupt communication during specific intervals.
- **Deceptive Jamming:** Signals designed to mimic the legitimate communication system's characteristics, thus confusing the receiver into accepting corrupted data.

e. Size and Mobility

Jammers can be portable (e.g., handheld or vehicle-mounted) or fixed installations, depending on the application. Portable jammers are designed to be small and lightweight, offering flexibility for mobile operations, such as in military or law enforcement settings. Fixed jammers, on the other hand, are typically larger and have greater power, providing comprehensive coverage for an area or facility.

f. Thermal Management

Jamming devices, particularly high-power ones, generate substantial heat. Effective thermal management solutions, such as heat sinks or fans, are necessary to maintain device performance and prevent overheating, which could lead to device failure.

g. Frequency Hopping and Spread Spectrum

Advanced jamming devices may incorporate frequency hopping or spread spectrum techniques to make them more difficult to detect and counter. These methods involve rapidly switching between different frequencies or spreading the jamming signal over a broad frequency range to make it harder for countermeasures to filter out.

3. Use Cases and Operational Scenarios for Jammers

RF jamming devices have a wide array of applications across different industries. Below are some of the primary use cases:

a. Military and Defense

The most well-known application of RF jamming is in electronic warfare (EW). The military uses jammers to disrupt enemy communications, radar systems, and GPS devices to create tactical advantages. Jamming can disable the enemy's ability to coordinate attacks, navigate, or use surveillance systems, providing a strategic edge on the battlefield.

b. Law Enforcement

Jammers are used by law enforcement agencies in specific situations, such as preventing the remote detonation of explosives or disabling unauthorized drone operations in sensitive or restricted airspaces. Additionally, jammers may be used in covert operations to prevent the interception of communications.

c. Counter-Surveillance

RF jamming is used in counter-surveillance operations to prevent eavesdropping and wiretapping. In such scenarios, jammers may be deployed to create a "bubble" of interference around a specific area or individual to prevent unauthorized signal interception.

d. Protection of Critical Infrastructure

In industrial, government, and military facilities, RF jammers can be used to prevent unauthorized wireless communication or cyberattacks. For example, jamming could be used to block unauthorized Wi-Fi networks or to protect critical communications from malicious interference.

e. Personal Security

Portable jammers can be used by individuals to block cell phone signals in specific scenarios where privacy or security is a concern, such as during confidential meetings or to prevent location tracking.

4. Legal Considerations and Ethical Use of Jamming Technology

While RF jamming technology has legitimate uses in defense, security, and testing, it is heavily regulated due to its potential to cause widespread disruption and safety concerns. Here are some important legal and ethical considerations:

a. Legal Framework

In many countries, including the United States, the use of RF jamming devices is restricted by law. The Federal Communications Commission (FCC) in the U.S. strictly prohibits the operation, sale, or marketing of any device that intentionally disrupts or interferes with lawful radio communications. Violations of these regulations can result in significant fines and criminal penalties.

b. Permissible Uses

Jamming devices may be legally employed by law enforcement and military agencies under specific conditions, typically with proper authorization. Some countries permit certain types of jamming for security purposes, such as in airports or correctional facilities, but strict regulations govern their deployment.

c. Ethical Considerations

The ethical use of jammers is closely tied to the potential consequences of their misuse. While jamming may provide security benefits, such as preventing terrorist attacks or enhancing privacy, it can also interfere with critical communications, including emergency services, aviation systems, and public safety communications. For this reason, RF jamming must be used responsibly and only in situations where the benefits outweigh the potential risks.

d. Countermeasures

As jamming technology advances, so do countermeasures designed to detect and neutralize jamming devices. These may include frequency-hopping techniques, signal encryption, or automatic reconfiguration of communication systems. Jamming devices must be designed with the understanding that these countermeasures may be employed by the target system.

5. Conclusion

RF jamming devices are powerful tools with a range of applications, from military defense to personal security. Understanding the technical specifications and design considerations is critical for building effective and reliable jammers. However, the legal and ethical implications of jamming technology must always be carefully considered, as unauthorized or indiscriminate use can have serious consequences. With proper knowledge and adherence to regulations, RF jamming devices can serve as valuable tools for protection, security, and testing in many industries.

Chapter 19: Advanced Signal Suppression Techniques

Signal suppression plays a critical role in minimizing unwanted interference and enhancing the performance of communication systems. As the complexity of modern RF and electronic environments grows, the need for sophisticated signal suppression techniques becomes more pronounced. This chapter explores advanced methods for signal suppression, including adaptive filtering, digital signal processing (DSP), ultra-low noise amplifiers, and cutting-edge active suppression systems.

1. Adaptive Filtering and Noise Cancellation

One of the most effective methods for suppressing unwanted signals is through adaptive filtering, particularly for noise cancellation in RF systems. Adaptive filters dynamically adjust their parameters to reduce interference from noise signals while maintaining the integrity of the desired signal.

a. Basics of Adaptive Filtering

An adaptive filter is a type of filter that changes its behavior in response to the input signal, aiming to remove unwanted noise while preserving the signal of interest. These filters use algorithms that continuously adjust the filter coefficients to minimize the error between the desired output and the actual output. Commonly used algorithms include the Least Mean Squares (LMS) and Recursive Least Squares (RLS) algorithms.

b. Applications in RF Systems

Adaptive filtering is particularly effective in environments where the interference is not constant or predictable. For example:

- **Noise Cancellation in Communication Systems:** Adaptive filters can cancel out unwanted noise from RF signals, such as interference from adjacent channels or power line noise, in real-time.
- **Speech Enhancement:** In communication systems such as VoIP or mobile phones, adaptive filtering helps to suppress background noise and enhance speech quality.
- **Interference from Multiple Sources:** In environments with multiple interference sources, adaptive filters can dynamically adjust to isolate the desired signal and suppress competing noise.

c. Techniques for Improving Adaptivity

- **Multi-channel Adaptive Filtering:** Using multiple sensors or antennas to capture different signals, multi-channel adaptive filtering improves performance by leveraging spatial diversity to filter out noise more effectively.
- **Neural Network-based Adaptive Filters:** Machine learning techniques, such as neural networks, can be used to improve the adaptability and accuracy of the filtering process, particularly in complex or dynamic environments.

2. Digital Signal Processing (DSP) for Signal Suppression

Digital Signal Processing (DSP) involves manipulating signals in the digital domain to suppress unwanted frequencies and enhance the desired signal. DSP provides powerful tools for both passive and active signal suppression, enabling real-time processing and adaptation.

a. Overview of DSP Techniques

DSP techniques used for signal suppression include:

- **Fast Fourier Transform (FFT):** FFT is used to convert signals from the time domain to the frequency domain. By analyzing the frequency spectrum of the signal, unwanted frequencies can be filtered out or attenuated.
- **Spectral Subtraction:** This technique involves estimating the power spectrum of the noise and subtracting it from the total signal spectrum, leaving only the clean signal.
- **Wavelet Transform:** Wavelet transform decomposes the signal into multiple frequency bands, allowing for selective filtering and noise reduction without distorting the signal.

b. Applications of DSP in Signal Suppression

- **Denoising:** In RF communication systems, DSP techniques can be used to filter out noise from weak signals, such as signals received in congested frequency bands or through noisy transmission channels.
- **Echo Cancellation:** DSP is widely used in telecommunication to cancel out echoes caused by reflections of signals in communication lines, improving signal clarity.
- **De-jittering:** In high-speed data transmission, DSP can remove jitter (variations in signal timing), ensuring accurate and stable communication.

c. Benefits of DSP for Suppression

- **Real-time Processing:** DSP systems can handle real-time processing of high-frequency signals, enabling immediate suppression of noise and interference.
- **Customizable Filtering:** DSP allows for the creation of custom filters tailored to specific noise types or interference patterns, providing a high degree of flexibility in suppression.

3. Ultra-Low Noise Amplifiers (ULNAs) in Signal Suppression

Ultra-low noise amplifiers (ULNAs) are designed to amplify weak signals with minimal additional noise, making them a crucial component in signal suppression. By minimizing the noise figure (NF), ULNAs allow for the extraction of weak signals from a noisy environment, effectively enhancing the signal-to-noise ratio (SNR).

a. Function and Design Considerations

The primary function of an ULNA is to amplify a signal without introducing significant noise. This is achieved by using high-quality components and minimizing the thermal noise introduced by the amplifier. Key design considerations include:

- **Low-Noise Transistors:** High-performance transistors with low noise figures, such as gallium arsenide (GaAs) or silicon-germanium (SiGe) technologies, are commonly used in ULNAs.
- **Impedance Matching:** To maximize signal integrity, ULNAs are designed to match the impedance of the input signal source, preventing signal reflection and loss.
- **Power Supply Considerations:** Power supply noise must be minimized to prevent unwanted signal interference, requiring high-quality, noise-free power sources.

b. Applications in RF and Communication Systems

- **Wireless Communication:** In wireless systems, ULNAs are used in the front-end receiver to amplify weak signals received by antennas, improving the overall sensitivity and performance of the communication link.
- **Satellite Communications:** ULNAs are often employed in satellite receivers, where signals from space are weak and need to be amplified without introducing significant additional noise.
- **Radar Systems:** ULNAs help improve the detection of weak radar signals, which is crucial for military and civilian radar applications.

c. Limitations

While ULNAs are effective at improving signal strength, they have their limitations. They typically work best in low-noise environments, and in systems with high levels of interference, additional noise suppression techniques (such as DSP or adaptive filtering) may be required.

4. Cutting-Edge Technologies in Active Signal Suppression Systems

Active signal suppression refers to technologies that actively generate counter-signals to cancel or reduce unwanted interference. These systems utilize real-time feedback and advanced algorithms to create an opposing signal that neutralizes the interference.

a. Antenna Arrays and Smart Jamming

Active suppression systems often use antenna arrays that can focus their energy in specific directions to cancel out interfering signals. Smart antennas dynamically adjust the phase and amplitude of the signals they emit, creating destructive interference with the jamming signal or noise.

b. Active Noise Cancellation (ANC)

Active noise cancellation is a technology widely used in consumer electronics, such as noise-cancelling headphones, and is now being adapted for RF applications. By generating a signal that is the inverse of the incoming noise, ANC systems can suppress low-frequency interference in communication systems.

c. Machine Learning in Signal Suppression

Machine learning (ML) algorithms are increasingly being employed in signal suppression systems. These algorithms can analyze signal patterns, predict interference, and dynamically adjust suppression techniques for optimal performance. This self-learning capability allows systems to become more efficient over time and adapt to new, previously unknown interference sources.

d. Dynamic Spectrum Management

In environments with dynamic interference, such as cognitive radio networks, active suppression can include dynamic spectrum management. This involves continuously scanning the available spectrum, detecting interference, and reconfiguring the communication system to avoid jamming or EMI by shifting to a cleaner frequency band.

5. Conclusion

Advanced signal suppression techniques are essential for maintaining the integrity and reliability of modern RF systems. By employing adaptive filtering, DSP, ultra-low noise amplifiers, and active suppression technologies, communication systems can operate efficiently even in the presence of significant interference. As the demand for more sophisticated and resilient RF communication grows, the continued development and integration of these advanced techniques will play a critical role in ensuring the reliability of both commercial and military communication systems. Signal suppression technologies not only enhance system performance but also enable the protection of sensitive data and the avoidance of costly disruptions caused by RF interference.

Chapter 20: Protecting Critical Infrastructure from RF Jamming and EMI

Critical infrastructure, ranging from power grids to military communication networks, is increasingly vulnerable to Radio Frequency (RF) jamming and Electromagnetic Interference (EMI). These systems form the backbone of national security, economic stability, and daily operations, making their protection from RF threats paramount. In this chapter, we will explore the vulnerabilities of critical infrastructure to RF interference, best practices for safeguarding these systems, and the role of RF shielding, encryption, and other security methods in countering these threats.

1. Vulnerabilities of Critical Infrastructure to RF Interference

The growing reliance on wireless communication and electronic systems for critical infrastructure has exposed several vulnerabilities. These systems are often interconnected, highly automated, and essential for maintaining public safety, health, and national security. As a result, they are susceptible to RF jamming and EMI, which can cause significant disruptions.

a. Power Grids and Energy Infrastructure

The power grid is increasingly controlled by digital systems and relies on wireless communication for monitoring and control. RF jamming can disrupt communication between grid components, causing blackouts or grid failures. EMI can also affect the performance of power plant sensors, transformers, and distribution systems.

b. Transportation Systems

Modern transportation systems, including trains, airplanes, and autonomous vehicles, rely on RF signals for navigation, communication, and control. Jamming of GPS or radio signals can lead to navigation errors, delays, and even accidents. EMI can interfere with the sensors and controls of automated vehicles, leading to malfunctions or accidents.

c. Communication Networks

Emergency communication systems, including those used by police, fire departments, and military, rely on RF for instant communication. RF jamming can disrupt these systems, compromising response times and coordination. Additionally, critical communication infrastructure may be affected by EMI, resulting in data loss or system failure.

d. Healthcare Systems

RF jamming and EMI pose significant risks to healthcare devices, particularly medical implants, diagnostic equipment, and hospital communication systems. Pacemakers, for example, can be disrupted by RF signals, while EMI can degrade the performance of imaging devices such as MRI machines and ultrasound equipment.

e. Military and Defense Systems

Military communication and navigation systems, radar installations, and weaponry are highly vulnerable to RF jamming. Electronic warfare tactics often involve the strategic use of RF jamming to disable enemy systems. This makes protecting defense infrastructure from both intentional and unintentional interference a critical priority.

2. Best Practices for Protecting Critical Infrastructure

Protecting critical infrastructure from RF jamming and EMI requires a multifaceted approach, including preventive measures, monitoring, and rapid response protocols. Below are some of the key strategies used to safeguard critical systems.

a. RF Shielding for Infrastructure Defense

One of the most effective ways to protect critical infrastructure is through RF shielding, which involves using materials or designs that block or absorb RF energy. Different shielding techniques can be applied depending on the type of infrastructure and its specific vulnerabilities.

- **Faraday Cages:** Faraday cages are enclosed structures made from conductive materials that shield equipment from external RF interference. These can be used to protect critical servers, communication hubs, and control centers.
- **Shielded Cables and Connectors:** Shielding cables and connectors in critical communication lines ensures that signals are not compromised by EMI or RF interference, protecting data integrity and system functionality.
- **Conductive Coatings:** Applying conductive coatings to sensitive equipment or infrastructure can help prevent external RF fields from penetrating and disrupting systems.

b. Grounding and Bonding Techniques

Proper grounding and bonding are essential for minimizing the effects of EMI. Grounding involves connecting the electrical systems of critical infrastructure to the earth, providing a path for unwanted electrical energy to dissipate safely. Bonding ensures that all metallic parts of the system are electrically connected, preventing differences in potential that could lead to electrical arcing or interference.

c. Electromagnetic Pulse (EMP) Protection

A specific form of EMI, Electromagnetic Pulse (EMP), has the potential to disrupt or destroy electronics and communications systems. Protecting critical infrastructure from EMP involves specialized shielding, surge protection devices, and hardening components against the effects of high-intensity electromagnetic fields. The use of EMP-rated surge protectors and installing faraday cages around critical control centers are common methods for mitigating EMP damage.

d. Spectrum Management and Monitoring

Constant monitoring of the electromagnetic spectrum is crucial for detecting and mitigating jamming attacks. By utilizing spectrum analyzers and monitoring systems, operators can identify unauthorized RF signals in real-time and take action to minimize their impact. Early detection systems can provide advance warnings of jamming attempts, allowing for countermeasures to be implemented swiftly.

e. Redundancy and Resilience

Redundancy ensures that critical systems can continue to operate even if one part of the infrastructure is compromised. For communication networks, this may involve having multiple frequency bands, backup power sources, and alternative communication methods in place. Redundant systems ensure that infrastructure remains resilient, even in the face of interference.

3. The Role of Encryption and Security Protocols

In addition to physical and technical defenses, securing communication systems through encryption is an essential strategy for protecting critical infrastructure from RF jamming and EMI.

a. Encryption in Communication Systems

Encryption ensures that even if an RF jamming attempt successfully interferes with the communication signal, the data remains unreadable to unauthorized parties. Encrypted communication channels prevent malicious actors from accessing sensitive information, such as control commands or data from surveillance systems.

- **End-to-End Encryption:** Ensures that data transmitted between endpoints is securely encrypted, even if the signal is intercepted or jammed.
- **Frequency Hopping and Spread Spectrum:** Techniques such as frequency hopping (where the transmission frequency rapidly changes) and spread spectrum (which spreads the signal across multiple frequencies) make jamming more difficult by making it harder for the jammer to lock onto a specific frequency.

b. Authentication and Authorization Protocols

Ensuring that only authorized users can access critical infrastructure systems is another layer of defense. By implementing strong authentication methods, such as multi-factor authentication (MFA), operators can prevent unauthorized access to critical systems that could be used to launch RF jamming or EMI attacks.

c. Signal Encryption for RF Jamming Defense

In cases where RF jamming is detected, the encrypted signal can be shifted to a secure frequency band or channel, rendering the jammer ineffective. This approach, often seen in military applications, enables systems to maintain communication even in the presence of interference.

4. Countermeasures for RF Jamming in Critical Infrastructure

When RF jamming is detected or suspected, rapid response and countermeasures are essential to protect infrastructure from disruption. Some of the most effective countermeasures include:

a. Signal Detection and Direction Finding

Advanced signal detection technologies can locate the source of RF jamming, enabling security personnel to quickly identify and neutralize the threat. Direction-finding antennas and triangulation techniques are often used to pinpoint the position of a jammer, allowing for a targeted response.

b. Jamming Countermeasures

Some critical systems are designed with built-in jamming countermeasures, such as automatic frequency shifting, which helps avoid interference by dynamically changing communication frequencies. Additionally, systems can be equipped with jamming detection algorithms that automatically switch to a backup frequency in case of an attack.

c. Geographic and Spectrum Diversification

By spreading critical communication channels over multiple frequencies and geographic regions, infrastructure can reduce the risk of being disrupted by a single jamming source. Spectrum diversification ensures that even if one part of the network is compromised, others remain operational.

5. Conclusion

The protection of critical infrastructure from RF jamming and EMI is a complex and evolving challenge that requires a combination of advanced shielding, robust security protocols, and adaptive countermeasures. As the world becomes more dependent on electronic and RF-based systems, safeguarding these critical systems from disruption becomes more crucial than ever. By applying best practices for shielding, monitoring, and encryption, and developing resilient systems that can detect and mitigate jamming and interference, infrastructure operators can ensure the continued functionality of critical systems, even in the face of deliberate or accidental RF threats.

In the next chapters, we will explore how these principles are applied specifically in military, defense, and communication systems, as well as how organizations can prepare for and mitigate the effects of RF jamming and EMI in their environments.

Chapter 21: RF Jamming in Military and Defense Applications

RF jamming, the intentional disruption of radio signals using electromagnetic interference, plays a pivotal role in military operations and defense strategies. It is used both offensively and defensively in electronic warfare to gain a tactical advantage, hinder enemy communication, and protect critical assets. As the nature of modern warfare evolves and military systems become increasingly reliant on complex RF communication networks, understanding RF jamming's strategic application and countermeasures is essential for maintaining superiority in the electromagnetic spectrum.

This chapter explores the strategic use of RF jamming in military applications, the countermeasures used to protect defense systems, and the broader implications of electronic warfare on military communication.

1. The Strategic Use of RF Jamming in Military Operations

RF jamming is a core tactic in electronic warfare (EW), which aims to disrupt or deny the use of the electromagnetic spectrum to adversaries. Military forces rely heavily on RF communications for everything from battlefield coordination to surveillance, navigation, and remote control of unmanned systems. RF jamming provides a means of disabling or degrading these systems, rendering them ineffective or unreliable in critical moments.

a. Offensive RF Jamming

Offensive jamming is used to disrupt or deny enemy communication, radar, and sensor systems. Key applications include:

- **Disrupting Command and Control (C2):** RF jamming can prevent an enemy from communicating within their command and control network, leading to confusion, disorganization, and the breakdown of tactical coordination. For example, disrupting military radio networks, satellite communications, or secure data transmission can severely degrade operational effectiveness.
- **Radar Jamming:** Military radars, essential for navigation, targeting, and surveillance, are prime targets for jamming. Techniques like deceptive jamming and noise jamming are employed to confuse enemy radar systems, rendering them unable to accurately detect or track objects, such as incoming missiles or aircraft.
- **GPS Jamming and Spoofing:** Global Positioning System (GPS) signals are crucial for modern military operations. Jamming or spoofing GPS signals can cause navigation systems to malfunction, leading to loss of positioning data and disrupting navigation for both ground and aerial forces.

b. Defensive RF Jamming

Defensive RF jamming is used to protect friendly forces from enemy interference. A military unit might use jamming to block incoming jamming signals or neutralize the effects of enemy attacks on its communication systems. Key defensive strategies include:

- **Anti-jamming Technologies:** Military systems are designed to resist RF jamming through advanced techniques such as frequency hopping (changing the transmission frequency rapidly) and spread-spectrum methods. These technologies make it more difficult for an adversary to target and disrupt communication channels.
- **Signal Diversity and Redundancy:** Multiple communication channels, frequencies, and methods are employed to ensure redundancy. Even if one frequency is jammed, alternative channels can keep the system functional, maintaining mission-critical communications.

2. Countermeasures Against RF Jamming in Defense Systems

While RF jamming is an effective tactic, defense systems have evolved to counteract these threats through a variety of strategies, both passive and active.

a. Frequency Hopping and Spread Spectrum Technologies

One of the most effective countermeasures to jamming is the use of **frequency hopping** or **spread spectrum** techniques. These technologies make the targeted signal appear on multiple frequencies or rapidly switch between frequencies, making it difficult for a jammer to lock onto a single transmission. For example:

- **Frequency Hopping:** Military radios and GPS systems use frequency hopping to avoid jamming. The signal jumps to a different frequency at regular intervals, and only the receiver with the correct hopping pattern can decode the message.
- **Spread Spectrum:** This technique spreads the signal across a wide bandwidth, effectively masking it within a sea of noise. Even if a jammer disrupts part of the frequency, the signal can still be decoded by the receiver over the remaining bandwidth.

b. Directional Antennas and Adaptive Filtering

Directional antennas allow military communication systems to focus their transmission or reception in a specific direction, reducing the chances of interference from unintended sources. Coupled with **adaptive filtering** technology, these systems can dynamically adjust their parameters to cancel out unwanted signals and isolate the target signal from jamming noise.

c. Electronic Countermeasures (ECM)

ECM systems are employed to detect and neutralize jamming efforts. These systems can:

- **Detect Jamming Sources:** ECM equipment constantly monitors the RF spectrum for signs of interference. Once a jammer is detected, the system can automatically deploy countermeasures, such as shifting to another frequency or activating an anti-jamming mode.
- **Signal Restoration:** Some advanced ECM systems not only detect jamming but also attempt to restore the original signal by filtering out the jamming noise.

d. Advanced Communication Protocols

To further reduce vulnerability to RF jamming, the military employs **secure communication protocols** that are resistant to interception and disruption. Techniques such as **encryption** and **error correction coding** ensure that even if a signal is intercepted or disrupted, it remains secure and intelligible to the receiver.

3. Electronic Warfare (EW) and Its Impact on Military Communication

Electronic warfare encompasses a broader strategy than just jamming. It involves the use of electromagnetic energy to attack or defend against enemy forces through disruption, deception, and denial of the electromagnetic spectrum.

a. Offensive Electronic Warfare

Offensive EW can include:

- **Jamming and Spoofing:** Disrupting or deceiving enemy radar, navigation, and communication systems.
- **Cyber-Electromagnetic Warfare (CEMW):** This integrates cyber operations with electronic warfare. For instance, a cyberattack may be used in conjunction with RF jamming to disable an enemy's digital infrastructure while simultaneously preventing them from communicating or detecting the attack.

b. Defensive Electronic Warfare

Defensive EW involves protecting friendly forces from enemy RF jamming and interference. The goal is to maintain secure communications while denying the enemy the ability to attack or disrupt friendly systems. Defensive strategies include:

- **Hardening Communication Systems:** Specially designed equipment and systems that can endure jamming attempts and continue functioning under electromagnetic duress.
- **Signal Restoration and Recovery:** Technologies that can recover or restore communication signals even after they have been partially disrupted by jamming.

c. EW and Multidomain Operations

Modern warfare increasingly involves multidomain operations, where electronic warfare is integrated with cyber, air, land, and space operations. The ability to jam enemy signals or protect one's own communications across all domains is crucial for maintaining superiority in complex, multifaceted combat environments.

4. Developing Resilient Systems in Defense Environments

Given the critical importance of RF communication in military operations, building resilient systems capable of withstanding RF jamming is a high priority for defense organizations. Several principles are being adopted to create more robust military systems:

a. Survivability Through Diversity

Diversity in communication methods is a key strategy for ensuring survivability in jamming-prone environments. By using a mix of communication modes—such as satellite, radio, microwave, and optical systems—military forces can ensure that, even if one system is compromised, others remain operational.

b. Redundant Systems and Backups

Military systems are increasingly being designed with built-in redundancy, allowing for automatic failover to backup systems in the event of a jamming attack. This can include backup communication channels, power supplies, and network infrastructures that ensure continuity of operations during interference.

c. Real-Time Threat Detection and Response

Modern military systems are equipped with real-time threat detection mechanisms that constantly monitor the electromagnetic spectrum for signs of potential jamming or other disruptions. Once a threat is identified, countermeasures are deployed automatically or manually to minimize the impact on operations.

5. Conclusion

RF jamming is a powerful tool in modern warfare, enabling both offensive and defensive actions in the electronic warfare domain. Its strategic use in disrupting enemy communication, radar, and navigation systems is critical for gaining and maintaining a tactical advantage. However, the development of advanced countermeasures, including frequency hopping, adaptive filtering, and electronic countermeasures, has made it increasingly difficult for jammers to effectively interfere with military operations.

As military forces continue to operate in an increasingly complex electromagnetic environment, building resilient systems that can withstand RF jamming and other electronic warfare tactics is essential. The integration of advanced technologies, diverse communication methods, and real-time threat detection will ensure that military communication systems remain secure, reliable, and capable of supporting operations in the face of electronic threats.

In the next chapter, we will explore how the principles of RF jamming, EMI control, and signal suppression can be applied to civilian and commercial environments, and how organizations can build careers in the field of EMI control and RF protection.

Chapter 22: Building a Career in EMI, RF Shielding, and Signal Suppression

The fields of Electromagnetic Interference (EMI), RF shielding, and signal suppression are becoming increasingly important as our world becomes more interconnected and reliant on electronic systems. As industries continue to develop and deploy high-tech systems for communication, navigation, defense, and more, the need for professionals who can protect these systems from EMI and RF jamming is growing. Whether you're interested in working for aerospace companies, defense contractors, or in telecommunications, mastering these technologies can open a wide range of career opportunities.

This chapter will guide you through the key skills, certifications, job roles, and networking strategies required to build a successful career in the EMI, RF shielding, and signal suppression industries. Additionally, we will explore how the field is evolving and how to stay ahead of emerging trends.

1. Key Skillsets for a Career in EMI, RF Shielding, and Signal Suppression

Building a career in EMI, RF shielding, and signal suppression requires a blend of technical knowledge, practical experience, and a deep understanding of electromagnetic theory. Below are the essential skills for entering and advancing in these fields:

a. Technical Expertise in Electromagnetic Theory

A solid understanding of electromagnetic theory forms the backbone of any career in RF and EMI control. This includes:

- **Electromagnetic Fields and Waves:** Knowledge of how electromagnetic waves propagate, how they interact with different materials, and how they can be manipulated or shielded.
- **Signal Transmission and Reception:** Understanding how RF signals behave, how interference affects signal integrity, and methods to mitigate it.
- **EMI/EMC Principles:** The ability to identify sources of EMI, analyze interference problems, and design solutions to prevent or minimize interference.

b. RF Engineering and Circuit Design

Working with RF systems often requires expertise in RF circuit design, including:

- **Transmission Lines:** Understanding the principles of impedance matching, wave propagation, and how RF signals travel through different materials and mediums.
- **RF Filters and Amplifiers:** Knowledge of how to design, implement, and troubleshoot RF filters, amplifiers, and other components critical for EMI control and signal suppression.
- **Shielding Techniques:** Skills in selecting and applying appropriate shielding materials and designing enclosures that protect sensitive electronics from EMI.

c. Testing and Measurement Techniques

Hands-on experience with testing equipment and methods is crucial. This includes:

- **Spectrum Analyzers and Oscilloscopes:** Proficiency in using these tools to analyze frequency spectra, signal integrity, and detect sources of EMI.
- **EMI Testing:** Understanding the regulatory standards for EMI/EMC compliance testing and how to apply these to real-world scenarios.
- **Simulations:** Familiarity with electromagnetic simulation tools, such as COMSOL, CST Studio, or ANSYS, to model and predict EMI behavior in systems and environments.

d. Problem Solving and Innovation

Given the dynamic nature of EMI challenges, strong problem-solving skills are essential. Whether it's identifying a source of interference, designing custom shielding, or developing new signal suppression techniques, being able to think critically and innovate is key.

2. Certifications and Training for EMI and RF Careers

To excel in this field, obtaining the right certifications and training will not only bolster your credentials but also enhance your practical skills. Here are some of the most relevant certifications and educational pathways:

a. Certifications

- **Certified EMC Engineer (CEng, EMC)** This certification is offered by professional organizations like the Institute of Electrical and Electronics Engineers (IEEE) or other national engineering bodies. It is recognized globally as proof of expertise in electromagnetic compatibility (EMC), including both EMI and signal suppression.
- **Certified RF Engineer (CFRE)** For those specializing in RF communications and shielding, this certification focuses on RF circuit design, signal integrity, and systems engineering. It's ideal for engineers working in wireless communications, aerospace, or telecommunications industries.
- **Certified Test Engineer (CTE)** This certification focuses on testing and measurement techniques for EMI/EMC, signal integrity, and RF systems. It is particularly useful for those working in product development or testing environments.
- **NARTE Certification** The National Association of Radio and Telecommunications Engineers (NARTE) offers certifications in EMC and RF fields. Their certification programs focus on testing, compliance, and troubleshooting EMI issues in real-world systems.

b. Formal Education

- **Bachelor's Degree in Electrical Engineering or RF Engineering:** A strong foundation in electrical engineering or RF systems is critical. Courses related to electromagnetics, circuit design, communications, and signal processing provide the necessary background.
- **Master's Degree or PhD in RF Engineering/EMC:** For those looking to deepen their expertise, a master's or doctoral program can offer specialized knowledge in advanced RF systems, signal suppression, and EMI analysis. Research opportunities in cutting-edge topics such as quantum electronics, photonics, and advanced materials for shielding can set you apart.
- **Workshops and Short Courses:** Many universities, as well as industry-specific organizations, offer short courses and workshops focusing on EMI/EMC testing, RF shielding design, and new materials for EMI mitigation. These can help you stay updated with the latest industry trends.

3. Job Roles in the EMI and RF Shielding Industries

As industries continue to integrate complex RF systems into their operations, the demand for professionals in EMI, RF shielding, and signal suppression is increasing. Below are some of the key job roles within these fields:

a. RF/EMC Engineer

RF/EMC engineers are responsible for designing, testing, and ensuring the compatibility of electronic systems with electromagnetic regulations. They work on everything from consumer electronics to aerospace systems, ensuring that devices and systems meet global EMI/EMC standards.

b. RF Design Engineer

RF design engineers focus on developing and improving RF circuits and systems, including amplifiers, oscillators, filters, and antennas. They play a crucial role in designing communication systems and ensuring that they operate without causing interference or being susceptible to it.

c. Signal Integrity Engineer

Signal integrity engineers specialize in maintaining the quality and reliability of signal transmission in high-speed systems. They address challenges like cross-talk, reflections, and electromagnetic interference, ensuring that signals are clean and free of distortions that could impair communication or data processing.

d. EMC Compliance Engineer

These engineers focus on ensuring that products and systems meet the regulatory requirements for EMI and EMC. They conduct testing, help with certification processes, and ensure that designs are compliant with local and international standards (e.g., FCC, CE, ISO).

e. Electronic Warfare (EW) Specialist

In defense applications, EW specialists work on jamming, anti-jamming, and countermeasure systems. These professionals design, test, and implement systems that can protect military and government operations from RF interference and jamming attacks.

f. Shielding Solutions Expert

Shielding experts specialize in designing and implementing RF shielding solutions for a wide range of applications, from consumer electronics to military-grade communications. They select materials, design enclosures, and integrate shielding techniques to protect sensitive electronics from EMI.

4. Networking and Growth Opportunities

Building a network and staying connected with professionals in the EMI, RF shielding, and signal suppression fields is critical for career advancement. Here are some strategies:

a. Professional Organizations

- **IEEE (Institute of Electrical and Electronics Engineers):** Joining IEEE provides access to a global network of engineers and researchers, opportunities for professional development, and access to cutting-edge research on EMI/EMC and RF systems.
- **EMC Society of IEEE:** This group focuses specifically on EMI/EMC issues and offers networking opportunities, conferences, and workshops.
- **Society of Automotive Engineers (SAE):** For those working in automotive applications, SAE provides a community for engineers to discuss EMI challenges and solutions in the transportation sector.

b. Industry Conferences and Workshops

Attending conferences such as the IEEE International Symposium on Electromagnetic Compatibility (EMC), the Applied Computational Electromagnetic Society (ACES) Conference, or the European Microwave Week is a great way to stay updated on industry trends, meet experts, and learn about the latest research and technologies.

c. Online Communities and Forums

Joining online communities on platforms like LinkedIn, Reddit, or specialized forums dedicated to RF and EMI topics is an excellent way to connect with peers, share knowledge, and learn about job openings, industry developments, and new technologies.

5. The Future of RF and EMI Control Careers

The future of RF and EMI control is bright, with emerging technologies in 5G, IoT, autonomous vehicles, quantum computing, and aerospace pushing the boundaries of what's possible in the electromagnetic spectrum. As systems become more complex and pervasive, the need for skilled professionals who can design, protect, and optimize these systems will only grow.

Key trends shaping the future include:

- **Advanced Shielding Materials:** New, lighter, and more effective materials are being developed to offer superior protection against EMI.
- **AI and Machine Learning in Signal Suppression:** AI algorithms are being used to detect, analyze, and mitigate interference in real time, revolutionizing the way systems handle EMI.
- **Quantum Technologies:** As quantum computing and communication technologies mature, new challenges and opportunities in EMI and RF control will emerge.

By developing the right skills, obtaining key certifications, and staying engaged with the latest trends, professionals in this field can look forward to a rewarding career with continuous opportunities for growth and innovation.

In the next chapter, we will dive into the tools and technologies used for EMI/EMC testing and explore how professionals can apply these tools to diagnose and solve interference problems in real-world environments.

Chapter 23: Tools and Technologies for EMI/EMC Testing

In the world of Electromagnetic Interference (EMI) and Electromagnetic Compatibility (EMC), testing is paramount to understanding and mitigating potential issues. Whether you are designing new products, troubleshooting interference in complex systems, or ensuring compliance with regulatory standards, effective testing tools and technologies are essential. This chapter provides an overview of the most important instruments and technologies used in EMI/EMC testing and how they can be applied to ensure that electronic systems perform as intended without causing or being affected by interference.

1. Introduction to EMI/EMC Testing

EMI/EMC testing is a critical aspect of electronics design, product validation, and regulatory compliance. The goal of testing is to identify sources of electromagnetic interference, assess how these sources impact the performance of systems, and implement measures to ensure compatibility. Testing also plays a key role in verifying that devices do not exceed regulatory limits set by authorities like the Federal Communications Commission (FCC), the European Union (CE), or other international bodies.

Key areas of focus in EMI/EMC testing include:

- **Radiated Emissions:** Identifying unwanted radiation from devices that can interfere with other electronic systems.
- **Conducted Emissions:** Measuring the electromagnetic energy that is conducted through power lines or cables, potentially affecting other equipment.
- **Immunity Testing:** Determining how well devices can tolerate external interference without malfunctioning.
- **Electromagnetic Susceptibility:** Assessing how external EMI sources affect the device's functionality.

Testing is typically done in anechoic chambers or specially designed labs to minimize external interference and ensure accuracy.

2. Instruments Used for Measuring and Testing EMI/EMC

To measure and analyze electromagnetic emissions and susceptibility, a variety of instruments are used. Each of these tools is designed to evaluate different aspects of EMI/EMC in specific ways.

a. Spectrum Analyzers

A **spectrum analyzer** is an essential tool for any EMI testing process. It is used to measure the power of electromagnetic signals across a range of frequencies. In EMI testing, spectrum analyzers help detect unintended emissions from a device under test (DUT) and visualize their frequency spectrum.

Key Functions:

- **Frequency Range:** Spectrum analyzers cover a wide range of frequencies, typically from a few Hz to several GHz, depending on the model.
- **Signal Power Measurement:** The analyzer measures the amplitude of the signal across the frequency spectrum, allowing for the identification of spurious emissions.
- **Real-Time Analysis:** Many modern spectrum analyzers allow for real-time analysis, which can be crucial in detecting intermittent or transient emissions.

Example Use Case:

b. RF (Radio Frequency) Analyzers

While similar to spectrum analyzers, RF analyzers are specifically designed to assess RF signals and their interactions with different devices. RF analyzers often provide higher precision in the analysis of RF properties such as modulation, bandwidth, and signal quality.

Key Functions:

- **Signal Modulation Analysis:** Useful for assessing signal integrity, modulation schemes, and bandwidth usage.
- **High Sensitivity and Accuracy:** RF analyzers offer very high sensitivity, helping to detect even the faintest emissions or signals.
- **Time Domain Analysis:** RF analyzers can perform both frequency and time-domain analysis, making them versatile in assessing EMI and EMC characteristics.

Example Use Case:

c. Oscilloscopes

An **oscilloscope** is one of the most common instruments used for real-time signal measurement and analysis. It is essential for observing the waveform of electrical signals, especially transient signals that could be causing EMI.

Key Functions:

- **Waveform Display:** Oscilloscopes display the waveform of electrical signals, helping engineers see transient spikes or irregularities that could indicate EMI problems.
- **Time Domain Analysis:** This is particularly important for understanding the timing of signal interference and identifying transient or pulse-like emissions.
- **Signal Capture:** Modern oscilloscopes can capture and store signals for later analysis, especially useful for studying sporadic or brief emissions.

Example Use Case:

d. EMI Receivers

An **EMI receiver** is specifically designed for testing radiated and conducted emissions from electronic devices. These receivers are highly sensitive, calibrated instruments used for compliance testing according to international standards such as CISPR (Comité International Spécial des Perturbations Radioélectriques).

Key Functions:

- **Emission Detection:** EMI receivers are capable of detecting both radiated and conducted emissions from devices and systems.
- **Frequency Scanning:** EMI receivers can scan through a wide frequency range, identifying both continuous and transient emissions.
- **Compliance Testing:** These instruments can perform automated testing to verify that devices meet EMC regulatory standards.

Example Use Case:

e. Anechoic Chambers

An **anechoic chamber** is a specialized environment designed to eliminate reflections of electromagnetic waves. The chamber is lined with materials that absorb RF signals, allowing for more accurate measurement of radiated emissions.

Key Functions:

- **Isolation from External Interference:** Anechoic chambers are isolated from external electromagnetic sources, ensuring that the tests are unaffected by outside interference.
- **Controlled Environment for Testing:** The chamber provides a controlled environment where devices can be tested for radiated emissions, without the influence of ambient electromagnetic noise.

Example Use Case:

f. Conducted Emission Test Systems

For testing conducted emissions, specialized test equipment is used to simulate power-line coupling and measure the conducted interference that travels along cables, power lines, or other conductors.

Key Functions:

- **Line Impedance Stabilization Network (LISN):** This is used to separate the device under test (DUT) from the power source and measure the conducted emissions on power lines.
- **Automated Testing:** Many systems are automated, providing detailed reports on whether a device exceeds the regulatory limits for conducted emissions.

Example Use Case:

3. Simulation Software for EMI/EMC Analysis

While physical testing is crucial, simulation software plays a key role in designing and analyzing systems before physical testing. Simulation tools can help engineers predict and mitigate EMI problems during the design phase, reducing the risk of costly design changes later.

a. Electromagnetic Simulation Software

Software tools like **COMSOL Multiphysics**, **ANSYS HFSS**, and **CST Studio** are used for modeling the electromagnetic behavior of systems, components, and devices. These tools simulate the impact of different materials, geometries, and configurations on electromagnetic fields.

Key Functions:

- **Field Simulation:** These tools simulate the electric and magnetic fields in a given environment, helping engineers understand how EMI might affect or be radiated from components.
- **Signal Integrity:** Engineers can assess the potential for signal degradation and interference in high-speed circuits.
- **Design Optimization:** Simulation allows for optimizing designs to reduce EMI, improving both performance and compliance with EMC regulations.

Example Use Case:

b. Circuit Simulation Tools

In addition to full-scale EM simulation, circuit simulation tools like **SPICE** (Simulation Program with Integrated Circuit Emphasis) are used to simulate signal integrity and EMI within circuits. These tools help analyze how different components in a circuit might affect each other in terms of emissions and noise.

Key Functions:

- **Noise Analysis:** SPICE simulations can identify sources of noise or interference in a circuit before hardware testing.
- **EMI Filter Design:** Engineers use SPICE to design and optimize filters that mitigate EMI within circuits.

Example Use Case:

4. Interpreting EMI Test Results and Corrective Measures

Once testing is completed, interpreting the results is the next crucial step. It's important to determine whether the device passes the required standards or if adjustments need to be made. If a device fails to meet EMI standards, engineers can take various corrective actions, such as:

- **Improving Shielding:** Adding or optimizing shielding materials to prevent emissions.
- **Filtering:** Adding passive components like capacitors, inductors, and resistors to suppress unwanted signals.
- **Layout Modifications:** Adjusting the layout of circuits and components to minimize the loop areas that radiate EMI.

In the next chapter, we will explore best practices for protecting personal devices from EMI and RF interference, along with DIY techniques for basic RF shielding in everyday environments.

Chapter 24: Best Practices for Everyday RF Protection

In today's increasingly connected world, the presence of electromagnetic fields (EMF) and radio frequency (RF) interference is virtually unavoidable. From cell phones and Wi-Fi routers to microwave ovens and electric vehicles, many common devices emit RF signals that can cause interference or pose potential health risks if not properly managed. In this chapter, we'll explore how individuals can protect themselves from the everyday effects of RF interference, offering practical steps to minimize exposure and secure personal devices against unwanted signals.

1. Understanding Everyday RF Exposure

RF signals are used in many modern technologies, and their ubiquitous presence is part of daily life. While most devices emit RF signals to perform their functions—such as enabling wireless communication or providing power—these signals can interfere with each other or disrupt other equipment. Additionally, prolonged exposure to certain RF frequencies has raised health concerns, particularly in relation to devices like cell phones and Wi-Fi routers.

Sources of RF in Daily Life:

- **Mobile Phones & Tablets:** Constant communication through cellular networks, Wi-Fi, Bluetooth, and GPS.
- **Wi-Fi Routers & Bluetooth Devices:** Wireless communication systems operating in the 2.4 GHz and 5 GHz bands.
- **Microwave Ovens:** Emitting RF waves to heat food, these devices can cause interference with other electronic systems.
- **Smart Home Devices:** Voice assistants, smart bulbs, and security cameras that operate on RF signals.
- **Electric Cars & Charging Stations:** Charging systems and vehicle electronics may emit RF signals that affect nearby equipment.

The goal of RF protection at the personal level is to minimize exposure and mitigate interference without sacrificing functionality or convenience.

2. How to Protect Personal Devices from EMI and RF Interference

Whether you're concerned about potential health effects or simply looking to ensure your devices work without interference, there are several practical steps you can take.

a. Using RF Shielding Materials

One of the most effective ways to protect sensitive devices from RF interference is by using shielding materials. Shielding can block or attenuate unwanted RF signals, preventing them from entering or escaping an area.

Faraday Cages:

Example:

Conductive Coatings and Foils:

Example:

Specialty Fabrics:

Example:

b. Minimizing RF Exposure at Home or Office

While shielding is one option, reducing exposure is also essential in spaces where RF interference can disrupt devices or health. Below are some steps that can be taken to minimize RF exposure at home or the office:

- **Move Devices Away from Work or Sleep Areas:** Keep RF-emitting devices such as Wi-Fi routers, baby monitors, and microwave ovens away from areas where you spend a lot of time. Position Wi-Fi routers in areas that are less frequently used, such as hallways or closets, to reduce exposure in bedrooms or living spaces.
- **Disable Unused Wireless Features:** Many devices, including laptops, smartphones, and even appliances like refrigerators, have wireless features that can be turned off when not in use. Disable Bluetooth, Wi-Fi, or GPS when you're not actively using these functions to minimize the device's RF emissions.
- **Use Airplane Mode on Phones:** When you don't need to communicate via cellular networks, Wi-Fi, or Bluetooth, activate airplane mode. This disables the RF transmitter in the device, reducing exposure to RF signals.
- **Use Wired Connections:** Whenever possible, opt for wired alternatives to wireless connections. For example, use Ethernet cables instead of Wi-Fi for internet connectivity, and use wired headphones instead of Bluetooth to reduce RF exposure.
- **Opt for Wired or Shielded Keyboards and Mice:** Some wireless peripherals emit RF signals. Using wired alternatives or those with built-in RF shielding can reduce your exposure to these signals.

c. Reducing RF Interference in the Environment

While shielding and minimizing exposure can help reduce the impact of RF interference, addressing the sources of interference is just as important. Some practical solutions include:

- **Proper Device Placement:** Arrange your devices to minimize interference. Avoid placing RF-emitting devices too close to each other, especially when using sensitive equipment such as radios, televisions, or medical devices.
- **Use of Power Line Filters:** Power lines can carry EMI from household devices or external sources. Power line conditioners and filters can help mitigate the impact of this interference, especially for sensitive electronics like audio equipment, computers, or televisions.
- **Wi-Fi Channel Optimization:** Many Wi-Fi networks are prone to interference due to crowded frequency bands, especially in densely populated areas. Tools such as Wi-Fi analyzers can help determine the least congested channel and improve signal strength.
- **Upgrade Your Electronics:** Older devices may not have adequate shielding or filtering, making them more prone to emitting or being affected by RF interference. Upgrading your devices to newer models with better EMI/EMC protection can significantly reduce issues with interference.

3. Best Practices for Securing Wireless Communication Networks

With the rise of IoT devices and smart homes, securing wireless networks is a crucial aspect of everyday RF protection. Not only do you need to protect against interference, but also against unauthorized access or hacking.

a. Use Strong Encryption on Wi-Fi Networks

One of the most fundamental steps to secure your wireless network is to use strong encryption. Enable WPA3 encryption (or WPA2 as a minimum) on your Wi-Fi router to protect your network from unauthorized access. Avoid using WEP (Wired Equivalent Privacy), which is easily compromised.

Change Default Router Settings:

b. Implement Network Segmentation

Segment your wireless network into different zones for various devices. For instance, you could have one network for personal devices like smartphones and laptops, another for smart home devices like thermostats and cameras, and another for guest access. This limits the potential impact of an RF vulnerability in one zone affecting the others.

c. Use VPNs and Firewalls for Enhanced Privacy

To protect your data while using Wi-Fi, consider using a Virtual Private Network (VPN). A VPN encrypts all internet traffic, shielding your communications from external eavesdropping, whether over public or private Wi-Fi.

Additionally, configure firewalls on your router and connected devices to block unauthorized connections and reduce the risk of cyber threats.

d. Secure Bluetooth Connections

Bluetooth-enabled devices can be vulnerable to hacking if not properly secured. Always use the "Pairing" feature, which requires manual intervention, and avoid leaving Bluetooth on when it is not in use.

Bluetooth Low Energy (BLE) Devices:

4. DIY Techniques for Basic RF Shielding at Home or Office

For individuals who wish to create simple, cost-effective RF shielding solutions, there are a few DIY techniques that can be employed:

- **Foil Shielding:** Wrapping small devices in aluminum foil can create a rudimentary Faraday cage to block RF signals. Ensure the device is fully enclosed to be effective.
- **Window Films:** Special RF-blocking window films are available that can block out unwanted external RF signals, particularly useful for individuals living near high-interference sources like cell towers or power lines.
- **Cell Phone Cases:** Many commercially available phone cases are designed to reduce RF exposure. These cases typically use materials like aluminum or copper mesh to shield the phone from radiation.
- **RF Blocking Curtains:** For areas like bedrooms or offices, installing curtains made from conductive materials can provide an additional layer of protection against RF signals from external sources.

5. Raising Awareness of RF Risks

Beyond technical protection measures, raising awareness of the risks associated with RF interference and exposure is important for promoting healthier practices. Engaging with local communities, schools, or workplaces to share information about RF exposure and best practices can foster a culture of safer, more mindful technology use.

Conclusion

While RF interference and electromagnetic exposure are inevitable in today's high-tech world, there are numerous practical steps individuals can take to protect themselves and their devices. By employing shielding techniques, minimizing exposure, and securing wireless networks, you can significantly reduce the potential risks associated with RF interference in everyday life. Whether you are concerned about personal health or the performance of your devices, these best practices provide the tools and knowledge to safeguard your environment and ensure the reliable operation of your electronics.

Chapter 25: Conclusion: The Future of RF Jamming, EMI, and Shielding

In an era defined by rapid technological innovation and ever-increasing reliance on wireless communication, understanding and mastering RF jamming, electromagnetic interference (EMI), RF shielding, and signal suppression is essential. As we've seen throughout this book, these technologies have become critical to the functioning and protection of communication systems across various sectors—whether it's for safeguarding military operations, protecting critical infrastructure, or ensuring the integrity of everyday devices. The future of RF protection is just as dynamic as the challenges it seeks to mitigate, and the next steps for advancement are both exciting and complex.

1. The Ongoing Evolution of RF and Electromagnetic Technology

Technological progress is the driving force behind the increasing importance of RF technologies. From the rise of 5G networks and the expansion of IoT to the development of next-gen electronic warfare capabilities, RF technology is at the core of modern communications, security, and defense. However, as RF signals become more pervasive and more devices rely on these signals, the risk of interference—whether accidental or intentional—grows exponentially.

- **Next-Generation Wireless Networks:** As 5G networks continue to roll out and beyond, the frequency bands used for communication will expand. These new frequency ranges—particularly in the millimeter-wave (mmWave) bands—offer increased data transmission speeds but also introduce unique challenges for signal integrity, shielding, and jamming. The increased density of 5G infrastructure, particularly in urban areas, will lead to higher levels of RF congestion, which can negatively impact performance.
- **The Expansion of IoT and Smart Devices:** As billions of IoT devices come online, from smart homes to industrial control systems, the number of RF signals in the environment will continue to rise. This influx of devices presents new challenges for maintaining clean communication channels and avoiding interference, particularly as the demand for seamless connectivity and low latency increases.

The drive toward higher-frequency, higher-speed RF communication presents both new opportunities and new threats. The systems that manage these technologies must evolve, with smarter jamming, shielding, and interference mitigation solutions coming to the forefront.

2. Emerging Challenges in the Field of RF Interference

With the rise of new RF technologies, new interference challenges are emerging. These challenges include not only the potential for interference in civilian sectors but also the evolving threats posed to national security and defense.

- **Adversarial Use of RF Jamming:** While RF jamming has been an essential tool for military operations, it is increasingly being used in non-military contexts. As RF technologies become more accessible, the potential for malicious interference—whether through terrorism, corporate espionage, or cyberattacks—grows. In the future, the ability to quickly and accurately jam communication systems will be a critical consideration for not only military defense but also cybersecurity professionals in both the public and private sectors.

- **Electromagnetic Spectrum Scarcity:** The electromagnetic spectrum is a finite resource. As new technologies demand more bandwidth—such as autonomous vehicles, smart cities, and augmented reality—the competition for spectrum allocation will intensify. This could lead to greater interference as more devices and services try to occupy the same frequencies, necessitating advanced methods of interference control, spectrum management, and RF shielding.

- **Health Concerns and Regulation:** The increasing awareness of potential health risks associated with RF exposure, particularly in high-density environments like 5G networks, will continue to be a point of contention. Regulatory bodies will need to carefully balance innovation with safety. As new research emerges on the effects of RF exposure, it will shape future regulations and standards.

3. The Future of RF Shielding and EMI Control

As RF interference becomes more complex, the technologies used to shield devices and control EMI must continue to evolve. The future of RF shielding and EMI control will be shaped by a combination of new materials, innovative designs, and advanced computational techniques.

- **Next-Generation Shielding Materials:** Traditional shielding materials like copper and aluminum have served their purpose for decades, but as RF technology evolves, so too must the materials used to shield sensitive equipment. Researchers are exploring new materials—such as carbon nanotubes, graphene, and metamaterials—that could offer superior shielding performance at smaller sizes and lighter weights. These materials could revolutionize how we protect devices from RF interference in the coming years.

- **Smart Shielding Systems:** The future of RF shielding could involve smart materials and adaptive shielding systems that can respond to changes in the electromagnetic environment. For example, advanced metamaterials could be engineered to change their properties dynamically in response to environmental factors, such as adjusting their conductivity in real-time to optimize shielding effectiveness.

- **Integrated EMI Mitigation in Devices:** With the rise of miniaturized devices, integrated EMI solutions will become more essential. Manufacturers will increasingly rely on embedded shielding technologies, such as conductive coatings or multi-layer circuit boards, to reduce the need for bulky external enclosures. This shift towards miniaturization will require a greater emphasis on designing systems for EMI resilience from the ground up.

4. The Role of Artificial Intelligence and Automation

Artificial intelligence (AI) and machine learning (ML) are already playing a significant role in the management and optimization of RF communication systems, and their influence is only set to increase in the coming years. AI will likely become integral in identifying, predicting, and mitigating RF interference, enabling more adaptive and dynamic approaches to shielding and signal suppression.

- **AI in Jamming and Countermeasures:** Smart RF jammers that use AI to dynamically adapt to changing environments are already in development. These systems can quickly assess and identify signals to jam, choosing the most effective strategy to disrupt hostile transmissions while minimizing collateral interference. As these systems become more advanced, they could provide highly targeted RF defense capabilities in both military and civilian applications.
- **Autonomous EMI Mitigation:** In complex environments with high levels of interference—such as in smart cities or industrial automation—AI-powered systems could continuously monitor RF spectra, predict interference patterns, and automatically adjust shielding or suppression mechanisms to maintain optimal performance. This level of automation could revolutionize how we manage RF interference in high-density communication environments.

5. Final Thoughts: Mastering RF Technologies for Reliable Systems

As we move into the future, mastering RF jamming, EMI, and shielding will require a multifaceted approach that incorporates cutting-edge materials, advanced computational techniques, and a deeper understanding of the evolving electromagnetic landscape. The ability to manage RF interference, prevent unauthorized jamming, and protect critical communication systems is no longer just a matter of technology; it is a matter of security, health, and operational reliability.

For engineers, researchers, and security professionals, the path forward will involve continuous learning and adaptation. By embracing emerging technologies and methodologies, we can stay ahead of the ever-growing challenges posed by RF interference, ensuring that our communication systems remain resilient, secure, and capable of supporting the next generation of technological advancements.

As we've seen throughout this book, RF protection and control are complex but indispensable components of modern technological systems. The pursuit of better shielding materials, smarter jamming techniques, and innovative EMI mitigation strategies will continue to evolve as the demands for clean and reliable communication networks grow. By mastering these technologies, we ensure that our systems—whether in defense, industry, or everyday life—are equipped to thrive in an increasingly electromagnetic world.

www.ingramcontent.com/pod-product-compliance
Lightning Source LLC
Chambersburg PA
CBHW082245220526
45469CB00009B/2877